18/24.

£3 −
ge−

Race Relations in Sociological Theory

RACE RELATIONS IN SOCIOLOGICAL THEORY

John Rex

Research Unit for Ethnic Relations,
University of Aston in Birmingham

ROUTLEDGE & KEGAN PAUL
London and New York

First published in 1970
Second edition published in 1983
Reprinted 1987
by Routledge & Kegan Paul Ltd
11 New Fetter Lane, London EC4P 4EE

Published in the USA by
Routledge and Kegan Paul Inc.
in association with Methuen Inc.
29 West 35th Street, New York, NY 10001
Photoset in Times by
Rowland Phototypesetting Ltd
Bury St Edmunds, Suffolk
Printed in Great Britain by
St Edmundsbury Press Ltd, Bury St Edmunds, Suffolk
Chapters 1–6 © 1970 by John Rex
Introduction and Chapter 7 © 1983 by John Rex

Library of Congress Cataloging in Publication Data

Rex, John.

Race relations in sociological theory.
   Includes index.
   1. Race relations.   I. Title.
   HT1523.R44 1982   305.8   82-12216

ISBN 0-7100-9299-7

Contents

Introduction to the Second Edition

The first edition of this book was written in 1967 and published in 1970. It is now republished because its argument remains largely valid within a limited literature on the conceptualisation of the field of 'race relations' within sociology. Nonetheless the original text was written at a particular intellectual and historical conjuncture, other arguments have been advanced in the ensuing twelve years, new encounters have occurred between ethnic and racial minorities, and my own views have undergone significant development. The development of my own argument has been set out in a set of essays published in 1973 as a result of my experience of a deteriorating race relations situation in Great Britain[1] and in a study of Handsworth, Birmingham conducted by Sally Tomlinson and myself between 1974 and 1978.[2] My more recent position was stated in an article entitled 'A Working Paradigm for Race Relations Research', originally published in *Ethnic and Racial Studies*,[3] which is reproduced here as Chapter Seven of this new edition. It will be useful, however, by way of introduction, to indicate the relationship of these new ideas to the original text.

The specific historical conjuncture which led me to write *Race Relations in Sociological Theory* was marked by the meeting of the UNESCO Experts Committee on the Nature

1. J. Rex, *Race Colonialism and the City*, Routledge and Kegan Paul, London, 1973.
2. J. Rex and S. Tomlinson, *Colonial Immigrants in a British City: A Class Analysis*, Routledge and Kegan Paul, London, 1979.
3. J. Rex, 'A Working Paradigm for Race Relations Research', *Ethnic and Racial Studies*, Vol. 14, No. 1, London, January 1980.

of Racism and Race Prejudice in 1967,[4] of which I was a member. That committee took as its starting point the conclusions of previous meetings of biologists that the concept of race as biologists used it had no relevance to the political differences among men and sought to indicate the kinds of sociological problems which were thought of as problems of race relations.

At that time the literature dealing with this problem was surprisingly sparse and this led me to offer my own tentative definition of the field. I suggested that this definition involved three elements:

(1) that it was a necessary but not a sufficient condition of a race relations situation that there should be a situation of severe competition, exploitation, coercion or oppression;

(2) that this situation occurred between groups rather than individuals, with only limited possibilities of mobility from one group to the other;

(3) that the intergroup structure so produced was rationalised at the ideological level by means of a deterministic theory of human attributes, of which the most important type historically had been based upon biological and genetic theory.

The first edition of the book dealt with all three of these elements. Chapters Two and Three dealt with the structure of colonial societies and Chapter Four with the position of immigrants and particularly colonial immigrants in a metropolitan society; Chapter Five dealt with the formal question of group and intergroup structure; and Chapter Six with the nature and institutionalisation of racist theory.

Necessarily a preliminary study of this kind offered an agenda for study rather than a set of final conclusions. Subsequently I have devoted my attention to the further implications of the problem of the structure of colonial society and to the position of colonial immigrants in metropolitan societies. In particular I have placed increasing emphasis on what I call

4. See M. Ashley, *Statement on Race*, Oxford University Press, London, 1972.

'class analysis'. This is integral to Chapter Seven of this edition, but some of the difficulties of the concept are set out in the theoretical appendix to *Colonial Immigrants in a British City*.[5]

Class analysis has been dominated by Euro-centric ideas deriving from the works of Marx and Weber. Although both Marx and Weber also dealt with imperial and colonial situations, the ideas which had most currency were those appropriate to an advanced capitalist society structured about the labour market and/or the exploitation of 'free labour'. The problematic was usually that of the encounter between proletarian and bourgeois in such societies and this problematic was extended to colonial societies with the participants looked at solely in their rôle as capitalist bourgeois and proletarian workers.

My own studies of colonial society were influenced by arguments about social and class structure in Latin America and the Caribbean,[6] by meeting the late Frantz Fanon, and by my continuing political engagement with the problem of the liberation of Southern Africa from white supremacy.[7] These studies led me to the view that the Euro-centric approach to these problems was limited and sociologically inadequate.

Marxism itself was, of course, increasingly conscious of the problems to which I refer. Wallerstein, building on the notion of the world economic system developed by Ferdinand Braudel, had recognised that the world economic system involved different relations between employer and employee

5. J. Rex and S. Tomlinson, *op. cit.*

6. Especially M. C. Smith, *The Plural Society in the British West Indies*, University of California Press, Berkeley 1965, but see also my earlier article, 'The Plural Society in Sociological Theory', *British Journal of Sociology*, Vol. X, No. 2, 1959 and my chapter 'New Nations and Ethnic Minorities' in *Race and Class in Post-Colonial Society*, UNESCO Paris, 1977.

7. See *Race Colonialism and the City* and 'The Compound, the Reserve and the Location – The Three Essential Institutions of South African Labour Exploitation', in *The South African Labour Bulletin*, Vol. 1, No. 4, Durban, 1971.

at the periphery from those which prevailed at the centre.[8] A number of other writers, such as Banarji,[9] Brenner[10] and Laclau,[11] also dealt with this question and with the related one of whether colonial society had to be understood in terms of a notion of a dual economy and society only partially penetrated by the capitalist mode of production.

Unfortunately, from the point of view of 'race relations' and indeed class theory, much of this argument was involved, largely as the result of the influence of Frank,[12] with a rather different question, namely that of economic development. The issue was imply that of whether colonial society allowed for development or whether underdevelopment at the periphery was the necessary concomitant of development at the centre. In so far as it dealt with class structure it did so in terms of the rôles of various participants in the world economic system. It tended to lack a historical dimension based upon colonial history and to fail to consider those aspects of men's relation to the economic and political system which did not arise simply from capitalist labour exploitation. Chapters Two, Three and Seven of this edition deal with some of these issues.

It will be clear from a reading of Chapters Two and Three that I recognise that the important structural issues in colonial societies are not simply those of class, whether in a Marxian, Weberian or any other sense. I speak there of the total images

8. I. Wallerstein, *The Modern World System – Capitalist Agriculture and the Origins of the European World Economy in the Eighteenth Century*, Academic Press, New York 1974, and F. Braudel, *Civilisation Matérielle et Capitalisme*, Armand, Colin, Paris, 1967.

9. J. Banarji, 'Modes of Production in a Materialist Conception of History', in *Capital and Class*, No. 3, London, 1977.

10. R. Brenner, 'The Origins of Capitalist Development – A Critique of Neo-Smithian Marxism', in *New Left Review*, No. 104, London, 1977.

11. E. Laclau, 'Feudalism and Capitalism in Latin America', *New Left Review*, No. 67, 1977.

12. A. G. Frank, *The Sociology of Underdevelopment and the Underdevelopment of Sociology*, Zenith Press, Copenhagen (undated), and *Capitalism and Underdevelopment in Latin America*, Monthly Review Press, New York, 1969.

of society referring to their own identity and that of other groups held by men and women in these societies and this includes, along with group formation arising from men's relations to the means of production, other factors such as men's legal status, their relation to political power, the bonding effect of ethnicity and the process of acculturation. In these chapters I sought to do full justice to the non-class elements involved, so much so indeed that some of my Marxist critics sought to classify me, along with M. G. Smith and others whose work I discussed, as a plural society theorist.

Chapter Seven makes it clear, however, that I do see value in emphasising class analysis as such. Indeed there, as in *Colonial Immigrants in a British City*, I define my own theoretical position as being almost wholly based upon class analysis. While other forms of grouping are recognised, their significance tends to be reinterpreted in class terms. Thus it is not solely because of the bonds of ethnicity that, say, East Indians in Guyana remain a distinct group but because men united in this way have been assigned a particular rôle in the economic, political and legal order.

In revising Marxian approaches to colonial society, moreover, I had originally placed great emphasis upon the historical dimension and on the original constitution of the colonial social system. This led to a picture on the one hand of basic economic institutions of what Weber called the 'booty capitalist kind' surrounded by a penumbra of ethnic estates such as 'free coloureds', 'poor whites', 'secondary pariah traders', 'free white settlers', 'missionaries' and administrators. That is to say it led to a relatively static picture of what I was increasingly inclined to call a colonial estate system.

Increasingly I came to realise, particularly after contact with Latin American colleagues at a UNESCO meeting in Mexico City, that this emphasis upon the historical dimension went too far. It gave only a picture of what might be called the 'archaic' structure of colonial societies. Actual societies, now often independent of their metropolises, were now actively involved in a process, albeit imperfect, distorted and incomplete, of capitalist development. My problem, however, was not simply to suggest that we should abandon the colonial type of analysis and replace it with a Euro-centric Marxian or Weberian one; it was that of doing justice to both elements.

I do not think that we are yet in a position as sociologists to offer a single general theory of colonial societies. What we can do is simply to indicate the variables involved in the construction of such a theory. I suggest, therefore, in Chapter Seven, that we should look both at those variables involved in the constitution of colonial social systems and at those involved in differing processes of development.

These variables are systematically set out in Chapter Seven. They involve, at the constitutive level, firstly, different pre-colonial social forms, secondly, different 'modes of production' or, more strictly, modes of economic exploitation, and thirdly, different stratification systems which organise the social as distinct from the purely economic division of labour. The development variables deal with variations in the process whereby political independence is attained, the process of economic liberalisation in which laissez-faire economic institutions succeed those of booty capitalism, the degree of incorporation of the former colonial society into the world economic order and the process of class struggle and revolution within the neo-colonial order. I believe that the understanding of societies as diverse as those of India, Africa, the Caribbean and Latin America depends upon the development of a typology of colonial social structures in which each type involves certain specific and historical values being given to each of these variables. We should then seek to develop a theory of the structure and development of each type.[13]

13. Although they have other theoretical interests and do not make any kind of class analysis central to their work, writers like Pierre Van den Berghe in *Race and Racism*, Wiley, New York, 1967, Richard Schermerhorn in his *Comparative Ethnic Relations*, Random House, New York, 1970, Philip Mason in his *Patterns of*

Theories of colonial and post-colonial societies such as these, however, deliberately accentuate the class element in structural analysis. Actual historical developments are likely to be affected by other elements. For this reason the new chapter should still be read in conjunction with Chapters Two and Three.

A different theoretical approach is necessary for the understanding of race relations situations engendered in metropolitan societies by the arrival of immigrant minorities from colonial societies. I have attempted to set this out in a number of subsequent essays (in chapters in Berting, Geyer and Jurkovich's *Problems in International Comparative Research in the Social Sciences* and Miles and Phizacklea's *Racism and Political Action in Britain*,[14] and in my book with Sally Tomlinson, *Colonial Immigrants in a British City*). In summary form this theoretical position may be stated as follows:

Metropolitan capitalist societies are understood as being structured politically and socially by a process of class struggle. So far as the native working class are concerned, this has led usually to a situation of a relative consensus based upon a truce. This consensus, which is sustained for relatively long periods, rests upon the acceptance by two class-based parties of the need for economic planning, the maintenance of relatively full employment, the existence of relatively free collective bargaining and the provision of a minimum of social welfare in terms of housing, health, education, social insurances and other services. In most European societies these rights have been won by labour and socialist parties based

Dominance, Oxford University Press, London, 1970, and Michael Banton in his *Race Relations*, Tavistock, London, 1967, all develop typologies of intergroup interaction in specific historical circumstances which have affected my thinking and the typology which I offer.

14. J. Berting, F. Geyer and R. Jurkovich, in *Problems of International Comparative Research in the Social Sciences,* Pergamon Press, Oxford, 1979, and R. Miles and A. Phizacklea, *Racism and Political Action*, Routledge and Kegan Paul, London, 1979.

upon the native working class, and immigrants may not necessarily be regarded as participating in the benefits of the truce. In the case of the United States of America, rights have been won by party machines based upon the more privileged immigrant groups, with Blacks, Chicanos and the native American people (American 'Indians') being late entrants, pressing their claims on the system.

This class model departs from a classic Marxian one in two respects. Firstly, it assumes that a truce of the kind described is possible for fairly prolonged periods. Secondly, it assumes that the class struggle expresses itself in a number of different struggles over the allocation of resources (e.g. struggles about the allocation of jobs, housing and educational opportunities). If, of course, the relative stability implied by the model were to end in conditions of economic crisis a different and more revolutionary pattern of class development would have to be envisaged but, at least until the onset of world recession in the late nineteen-seventies, it seemed to me that, in trying to estimate the structural position of colonial immigrant minorities, one could and should assume relative stability of the main class structure based upon the class truce.

My first empirical work with Robert Moore[15] concentrated on what we called 'housing-classes' and we sought to emphasise the role of the housing allocation system and the rights of groups within it in structuring relations between natives and immigrants. Later, in my work with Sally Tomlinson, I thought it useful to explore the relations between the housing system and the job market and educational systems. We then asked whether there was sufficient evidence of exclusion of immigrant minorities in work, housing and education to make them not simply a disadvantaged housing class, but more generally an underclass.

I do not wish to suggest that there is empirically a total underclass situation amongst immigrants in any of the ad-

15. J. Rex, and R. Moore, *Race, Community and Conflict*, Oxford University Press, London, 1967.

vanced capitalist countries. But it is still the case that there is sufficient concentration of these minorities in poor and insecure jobs, in inner-city ghettos and in underprivileged schools to make the ideal type of the underclass empirically relevant as a yardstick.

In using the term 'underclass', even on this ideal typical level, however, I have sought to modify the way in which it is used by Gunnar Myrdal.[16] Whereas Myrdal refers to the underclass as a hopeless mass left out of the opportunity structure of American society, conceived in liberal and individualistic terms, I have suggested that the position of the underclass should be compared with that of the working class incorporated in the welfare state and that it has the potential, using Marxian terms, to become an 'underclass-for-itself', that is to say, not to despair, but to organise both culturally and for political action.[17] Thus the immigrant minorities appear, in my work on Britain, as caught up in a complex and three-sided class struggle.

This kind of class analysis has not been generally acceptable to my Marxist colleagues. The question which they raise, however, is not a simple empirical one of whether or not, factually speaking, the immigrant minorities are in a different structural position from the majority of the working class. What they wish to argue is that whatever their present position and whatever the position of the native workers, the longer-term development of capitalist crisis must lead to changes in both and ultimately to working-class unity.

In part my answer to this is that such a theoretical projection is worth retaining but that it must be empirically proved. In part, however, I wish to raise more far-reaching issues. The ideologies and structures of the immigrant underclass appear to me to be based not simply upon false or true consciousness of their position in metropolitan society. They reflect the rôle of these minorities in the structure of the world economic

16. G. Myrdal, *Challenge to Affluence*, Gollancz, London, 1964.
17. See my footnote to Chapter One in Rex and Tomlinson, *op. cit.*

system or the structure of empire over four hundred years.

Increasingly, however, since my attention has been focussed on South Asian and Caribbean minorities in Britain, I have been forced to recognise the striking structural difference between Indian and Pakistani groups on the one hand, and West Indians and American Blacks on the other. The groups of Indians and Pakistanis whom I have studied are not simply to be defined negatively as poor immigrant workers. In fact they come from a variety of structural positions in Indian society and are bound together by differing ties of ethnicity, religion, language, nationality and culture as well as class and status. When one considers Jat Sikhs migrating in the first place to factory work, one is speaking of relatively well-off men owning land or aspiring to hold land and having had a particular historic and cultural rôle in India. They also have a special relationship both to other Indians and to the Ramgaria Sikhs who occupied an inferior rôle in the Punjab but gained considerably in power, wealth and status if they had lived and worked in East Africa.

This would appear to raise problems, moreover, not merely in relation to treating them as an underclass in British society, but also in relation to the applicability of our colonial estate model in post-colonial society. So far as the former is concerned, obviously much work has still to be done in developing an adequate theoretical perspective in relation to minorities who have the cultural and economic resources both to by-pass and to participate successfully in the class system of metropolitan society. Neither the Marxian nor the Weberian class model in its simple form is adequate to comprehend this. So far as the second is concerned, clearly my model of post-colonial society, based as it is largely on American and African material, has to be considerably extended to take account of the complexity of structure of the Indian Empire, the British Empire in India and the participation of Indians in the non-Indian British Empire. Van den Berghe has suggested,[18] in criticism of my work, that it would probably be best simply to treat the immigrant minorities which I have studied as 'ethnies', abandoning the claim to class analysis altogether. That may well be a possible terminological and theoretical strategy. I am inclined to believe, however, that if it is not tied to Euro-centric conceptions and if it allows for the complexity, structural and historical, of the relations which groups of men might have to positions of political and economic power in empire, class analysis may yet be useful in analysing minority problems both at the metropolitan centre and at the colonial periphery.

Whereas Van den Berghe presses me in a culturalist and biological direction, my Marxist critics would suggest that, both in the metropolis and in the colonial periphery, there is more to be gained from preserving more or less classical Marxian concepts of class (albeit as diverse as those used in Marx's writings on France in 1848) than in using the more eclectic concepts which I have suggested. This again is a possible theoretical strategy and I would not absolutely oppose work carried out in these terms. Whether it works will depend on the extent to which the capitalist world economic system has displaced other forms of economic and political structure. For my part, however, I see this process of displacement as still incomplete and partial and though I allow for 'incorporation in the world economic system' as one of my developmental variables, I see the dynamics of colonial social structure as still having other points of origin.

There are, of course, some situations which would yield more to Marxian analysis than others. This is particularly true where an advanced capitalist economy of the metropolitan type has been successfully implanted in the colonial periphery. This is certainly true of South Africa. Even here, however, the most committed Marxist theorists have been forced to concede that there is a problem in describing black

18. P. Van den Berghe, 'Races, Ethnicity and Class in Britain – a dialectical duel with the ghosts of Marx and Weber', in *Contemporary Sociology*, Vol. 9, Part 5, New York, 1981.

and white workers as part of a single working class.[19] Both clearly have their lives very largely determined by their rôle in the economic system, rather than by their ethnicity, colour or culture. But they may well still have different relationships to this economic system and behave differently as classes-for-themselves, and it is this type of differentiation which seems to require a more sophisticated type of class analysis than a Euro-centric Marxism is capable of providing.

Referring back to the threefold definition of race relations situations given at the beginning of this chapter, it is clear that most of what I have been saying refers to the first aspect of the definition. What I have been discussing are situations of 'severe competition, exploitation, coercion or oppression'. But I have been selective in the kinds of situation which I have discussed. There are situations of a similar kind in which individuals are exploited or oppressed as individuals, and there are situations in which the rationale for exploitation and oppression is not of a deterministic kind. The characteristic of race relations situations which occurs in the colonial context and when members of a metropolitan society encounter colonial immigrants as well as poor refugees is that both the element of group exploitation and oppression and that of the rationalisation of the system in terms of some sort of deterministic theory are present. This is the theme of Chapters Five and Six of the original edition.

This feature of race relations situations is what we missed in attempts to replace the notion of race with that of ethnicity. Wallman,[20] for instance, following Barth, emphasises that ethnicity is essentially situational and that, while it may sometimes be a liability, it may also be called upon as a resource. According to the approach adopted here, a race relations situation always implies that ethnicity is a liability

19. See, for example, H. Wolpe, 'The White Working Class in South Africa', in *Economy and Society*, Vol. 5, No. 2, London, 1976.

20. S. Wallman, 'The Boundaries of "Race" – Processes of Ethnicity in England', *Man*, Vol. 13, No. 2, London 1978.

for one of the groups involved. This is not to say that interethnic relations do not form a legitimate field of study. The notion, however, is a wider one than that of race relations.

It is difficult in fact to disentangle the themes of Chapters Five and Six. Groups are distinguished from one another and mobility between them is restricted partly, at least, by racist theory. Racist theory, on the other hand, only becomes possible when it can be applied to groups. Both, moreover, come into existence only in situations when one group has something to gain from the other's loss; that is to say in situations of exploitation and oppression.

Much, nonetheless, is to be gained from the study of the development and institutionalisation of racism. What Chapter Six seeks to show is that, even where explicit racist theory of the biological kind ceases to have credibility, it may nonetheless be institutionalised for instance in popular discourse and in the media and that such racist discourse involves implicit reference to theory of a more generalised kind. The existence of race relations situations therefore requires analysis of this discourse and the manner of its institutionalisation.

Finally, at the time of writing this introduction I should add that I have recently encountered two types of argument which lead me to have some doubts about the notion of class analysis as such, or at least suggest that it should be modified and refined. These are the arguments advanced by Van den Berghe in his important book *The Ethnic Phenomenon*[21] and by Charles Nixon in a paper on the concept of responsibility in the writings of Marx and Weber.[22]

Van den Berghe suggests that ethnicity involves the extension of the principle of nepotism which is inherent in human interaction. I think that this is probably true. It will always be

21. P. Van den Berghe, *The Ethnic Phenomenon*, Elsevier Press, New York, 1981.
22. C. Nixon, *The Concept of Responsibility in the Work of Marx and Weber*, unpublished paper to a conference in Duisburg, Germany, December 1981.

the case that men will promote the interests of those whom they see as their own against outsiders. But the question remains 'to whom is the protection of nepotism extended?' Clearly it is highly selective and on Van den Berghe's own analysis the fact of nepotism as a matter of biological survival is coupled with the notion of competition for resources and with that of hierarchy. It is thus within situations of economic competition and political domination that the principle of nepotism flourishes. I find that my own analysis has much in common with Van den Berghe's. Both of us are disinclined to give much credence to the operation of normative factors in the kinds of intergroup situation which we have been discussing, except as rationalisation of group interest. The new point which Van den Berghe sets against both the Marxian and Weberian type of class analysis is that alliances between individuals result not solely out of the rational perception of common interest but at least in part from a primordial tendency to advance the interests of those thought of as one's own. It seems to me that the recognition of this fact provides a valuable correction to the rationalism implicit in normal class analysis.

Nixon, on the other hand, seeks to place primary emphasis upon the notion of responsibility and group formation rather than on that of class. It seems to me to be correct to say, as he does, that in any empirical analysis it is the actual formation of groups capable of collective action which should have precedence over the quasi-group concepts of class. I have pointed out elsewhere that concepts like those of class refer not to actual group structures but to more generalised images of society arising on the ideological level[23] and I would support Nixon in directing attention back to the questions of group structure. Such analysis is essential in studying the formation of colonial society and other race relations situations. Nonetheless the generalised images which arise on the ideolo-

23. Theoretical Appendix to Rex and Tomlinson, *op. cit.*

gical level are still themselves a structural fact about these societies and situations. I believe that a sensitive use of the class-in-itself, class-for-itself problematic can take account of both group structures based upon the concept of responsibility as it is developed by Weber[24] and upon ideological elements which have potential for future group formation. The latter are especially important when images of social order appeal to the rhetoric of race.

It seems to me that it is against this theoretical background that we can look forward not so much to a single generalised theory of race relations but to theories of structure and development in post-colonial societies such as those in post-colonial situations in the Caribbean, the Americas, Southern Africa and Southeast Asia, as well as in situations of long-distance immigration from the colonial periphery to the metropolitan centre. It is in these situations that race has become a perplexing political issue overlapping with and sometimes displacing the issue of class.

---

24. I am referring especially to Weber's discussion of the concepts of 'group', 'representation' and 'responsibility' in Chapter One of the first volume of *Economy and Society*, Bedminster Press, New York, 1968.

1. The Theoretical Problem Stated

The problem of race and racism challenges the conscience of the sociologist in the same way as the problem of nuclear weapons challenges that of the nuclear physicist. This is not to say that sociology can dictate to men and nations how they should behave toward one another any more than that the nuclear physicist had some special competence to advise the American President whether or not he should drop the atom bomb on the Japanese. But it is to say that, in so far as whole populations have been systematically discriminated against, exploited and even exterminated, the sociologist might legitimately be asked to lay the causes of these events bare. The aim of this book is to provide a conceptual basis for doing this.

Conceptual discussion might well appear to some to involve fiddling while the gas ovens burn. Yet it is important to realise that sociology as a discipline has had some difficulty in coming to grips with this problem. The claim of the racists in the Europe of the nineteen-thirties was that race was a biological category, and that appeared to exclude sociological discussion. And, when the falseness of racist biology was systematically exposed, some sociologists were inclined to argue that the problem simply did not exist. Race was a category based upon some sort of false consciousness, and it was the duty of sociologists to reduce all statements about racial difference to statements about some other kind of socially differentiated structure, such as class. Only recently has the question been raised as to whether class really does have some kind of superior ontological status to race, and whether there is not a sense in which the 'race war' is not a more important central structural and dynamic principle in sociology than the class war.[1] A time has therefore arrived at which there is an urgent necessity for a reassessment of the rôle of the race concept in sociological theory.

It might perhaps be said that the fact that the concept of race and the problem of racism is primarily a problem for social science rather than for biology has been established in a quite uniquely authoritative way by a consensus of world experts. For, after the Second World War, UNESCO called together first a group of biologists and social scientists (in 1947) and then on two occasions groups of biologists (in 1951 and 1964), in order to give an authoritative opinion on the race question.[2] The biologists' final statement, made in 1964 and issued as the 'Moscow Declaration', represents the most up-to-date biological opinion on the subject. The full significance of this declaration can be assessed in the light of papers prepared for the Moscow conference and particularly from the introduction to these papers prepared by the Belgian biologist Jean Hiernaux, who has summarised the areas of agreement and disagreement among the experts.[3]

The biologists' conclusions are complex and technical and it would be quite beyond the scope of the present book to set them out in detail. Nonetheless it is important that we should in-dicate that they do not support certain popular conceptions as to the nature of race, which were systematically propagated by racist theorists, and which even today are widely accepted, even though they may not be so systematically rationalised as they were.

The popular conceptions to which we refer are as follows: first, that the differences in rights which exist between groups of men, within a nation, between nations and between groups

1. See, for instance, R. Segal, *The Race War*, Cape, London, 1966; R. Debray, *Revolution in the Revolution*, Pelican, London, 1968; F. Fanon, *The Wretched of the Earth*, Macgibbon and Kee, London, 1965.

2. UNESCO, Paris, *Statements on Race and Race Prejudice*, 1950, 1951, 1964 and 1967.

3. Hiernaux, Introduction: 'The Moscow Expert Meeting', *International Social Science Journal*, Vol. XVII, No. 1, 1965, UNESCO, Paris.

which are internationally dispersed, rest upon differences of behaviour and of moral qualities which are genetically determined. Thus the maintenance of a particular political order in the world is represented as being 'scientifically' determined, rather than being based upon force, violence and usurpation. Many subsidiary propositions flow from these basic ones, but they are the essential intellectual core of the racist position.

The general position adopted by the biological experts in Moscow is that the concept of race, and more generally of genetic inheritance, which they feel justified in using, gives no support whatever to these popular conceptions. But this is best understood if we look briefly at what it was that the experts actually said under the headings of the use of the concepts of race and population, the rôle of heredity and environment in determining human characteristics, the actual nature of intergroup differences, the single or multiple origin of the human species, the degree of independence or association between different traits, the rôle of biological and cultural factors in evolution, the consequences of intergroup marriage, the survival value of proved differences between populations, and the possible inheritance of psychic characteristics.

The principal conclusions reached on these points appear to be as follows:[4]

(1) Race is a taxonomic concept of limited usefulness as a means of classifying human beings, but probably less useful than the more general concept of populations. The former term is used to refer to 'groups of mankind showing well developed and primarily heritable physical differences from other groups'. The latter refers to a 'group whose members marry other members of the group more frequently than people outside the group' and hence have a relatively limited and distinctive range of genetic characteristics. In any case, however, whether we use the concept of race or population, the experts agree that human population groups constitute a continuum, and that the genetic diversity within groups is probably as great as that between groups.

4. *Ibid.*

(2) It is agreed that observable human characteristics are, in nearly all cases, the result of biological and environmental factors. The sole difference which could be attributed to biological heredity alone was that relating to blood-groups and the populations which shared the same blood-group by no means coincided with 'races' in the popular usage of the term.

(3) The various characteristics commonly grouped together as racial, and said to be transmitted en bloc, are, in fact, transmitted either independently or in varying degrees of association.

(4) 'All men living today belong to a single species and are derived from a common stock' even though opinions may differ as to how and when groups diverged from this common stock. Interbreeding between members of different groups is possible and productive and in 1964 as distinct from 1951 the experts saw a 'positive biological aspect of this process' (i.e. saw interbreeding as possibly beneficial from an adaptive point of view) 'while at the same time repeating the denial, at all events in the light of present scientific knowledge, of any negative aspect for mankind in general'.

(5) Taking into account the possibility of a looser usage of the term 'race' to refer to a national inbreeding population, it may not be desirable from a standpoint of combatting racism to deny that a particular national group may be referred to as a race, but rather to affirm that it is not justifiable to attribute cultural characteristics to the effect of genetic inheritance.

(6) Human evolution has been affected to a unique degree as compared with the evolution of other species by migration and cultural evolution. The capacity to advance culturally is one shared by all members of *homo sapiens* and, once it exists, is of far greater significance for the evolution of the species than biological or genetic evolution.

Taken together these findings point clearly to one single conclusion. The concept of race as used by the biologists has no relevance to the political differences among men, and since the whole notion of race and racism as it appears in popular discussion is concerned with these political differences, the question which we have to face is what the characteristics are of those situations which men call racial.

If the possibility of racial differences being biologically based is excluded, two other possible bases, neither of them necessarily sociological, might in principle be considered. One is that there are psychological differences between members of different racial groups, the other that the term merely refers to culturally distinct groups. Neither of these possibilities, however, provides an adequate explanation of how it is that men come to be classified as racially different.

Many problems arise in the attempt to assess psychological differences between races. There are few tests if any which are so free of cultural content as to permit comparisons between subjects drawn from different cultural backgrounds, and it would certainly seem to be the case here, as it is more generally with biological characteristics, that differences between individuals within the same population are at least as great as those between groups. In any case, however, it is somewhat difficult to see what could be meant by a purely psychological determination of intergroup differences divorced from the notion of differences of genetic inheritance. If psychic character is thought of as the consequence of the socialisation process then we should have to say (a) that a variety of types emerges from the socialisation process amongst all groups and (b) that insofar as socialisation processes do vary between cultures and produce differing distributions of the various personality types, the psychological determination of intergroup differences would appear to be dependent upon cultural differences.

So far as the cultural causation of intergroup differences in appearance, behavioural characteristics, institutions, psychic character and so on is concerned, no one would deny it. There certainly are different nations and cultural minorities within nations to be observed in the world. The question is whether the problem of the differences between these groups is coincident with the differences between groups which are said to be racial. Our answer to this question is that, although these cultural differences, or as it is sometimes said, differences between ethnic groups, may sometimes become the basis of a race relations structure and of a race relations problem, this need by no means always be the case. Our task then would appear to lie in discovering which of these culturally differentiated groups come to be thought of as races, and also what other types of groups are so classified.

It would appear to be the case that there are two observable features of any situation in which a problem of race is said to exist. One is the obvious one that the groups are called races, with whatever deterministic overtones that term might appear to have. The other is that there seem to be a definite and restricted number of social structures in relation to which in popular conceptions the term racial is used and in which there would appear to be a need for some distinctive sociological term. At this point we have to look at the problem of race sociologically.

Clearly the problem of a sociology of race relations is a peculiar one as compared with most other special sociologies. It starts with the task of unmasking false biological or related theories. Having done this, the question is what it has to do next. A few writers have taken the view that beyond this all the sociologist has to do is to show the consequences of such theories being held, so that phenomena like those connected with anti-semitism in twentieth-century Europe would be seen or studied simply as the consequence of the preaching of racist ideas. This, however, would appear to involve cutting off the investigation of a causal chain more arbitrarily than is common in sociology. We should surely look not merely at the consequences of racist theory, but also at its causes and at its functions.

Curiously sociologists, who on other occasions talk the language of functionalist theory, asking of every belief or other cultural item what function it has for a total social system, are inclined, when they turn to the study of race relations, to drop their systematic perspective. The view that racist beliefs might be explained in terms of function is associated with Marxist interpretations, which attribute racism to a ruling class attempt to justify its rule, and all such interpretations are thereafter dismissed as Marxism.[5] In point of fact, one very distinguished

5. M. Banton, *New Society*, April 3, 1969.

contributor to the whole debate about the sociology of race relations is the American negro Marxist, O. C. Cox,[6] but he is by no means alone in taking the view that racist theory and racialist practice arise in specific structural situations. Nor are he and other Marxists alone in holding the narrower view that racist beliefs have to do with stratification.

Before we begin a review of some of the major sociological theories which are relevant to the study of race relations, we should clarify a little more what it is exactly we are doing. We are trying to discover which of the various kinds of social situations, structures and processes which sociologists study belong within the sub-field of the sociology of race relations. Clearly there is some ground for agnosticism as to whether such a specific class of situations, structures and processes, and such a field study exist. But if we can show that there is a distinct group of social phenomena, with demonstrably different attributes from other phenomena (e.g. class), we shall have established our point.

What we have to do in the field of race relations is, of course, what Emile Durkheim suggested should be the sociologist's first step in any investigation. As he put it, the sociologist in approaching a new field of enquiry should 'investigate first of all by what characteristics one might recognise the thing so designated, then classify its varieties, investigate by methodical inductions what the causes of its variation are, and, finally, compare these results in order to abstract a general formula'.[7]

There is, however, a particularly difficult problem in defining the field of the sociology of race relations, which arises from the important rôle of beliefs in the very constitution of the phenomenon in question. A sociologist's work would indeed be much simpler were it possible to give something like an ostensive definition of his field. But the fact is that, unlike the natural scientists, who may be thought of as applying concepts to things, the sociologists seek to apply concepts to the understanding of

6. O. C. Cox, *Caste, Class and Race*, Monthly Review Press, New York, 1959.
7. E. Durkheim, *Rules of Sociological Method*, Free Press, Glencoe, 1950, p. 25.

social relations, and social relations in turn depend upon the conceptualisations which actors make of their world and of other actors. It is not possible therefore to make an absolute distinction between structures of social relations as they really are uninterpreted by participant actor's theories and concepts, and the ideas and concepts and theories in terms of which interpretations are made.

An example drawn from the work of one of the most important theorists we shall be discussing may serve to illustrate the sort of difficulty which we are apt to encounter. It concerns M. G. Smith's treatment of the meaning of colour in intergroup relations in the Caribbean.[8] Smith begins by recognising that one important subjective dimension in terms of which individuals categorise each other and orient their behaviour towards one another is that of skin colour. On investigation, however, it turns out that if a man has certain other characteristics such as high income, education, or a reputation for associating with people of lighter skin colour, he will be seen as whiter than he is.

Smith uses this fact in support of a general argument that the proper framework for Caribbean sociology is that which is provided by the plural or segmented society concept, rather than that which looks on Caribbean societies as exhibiting patterns of 'race relations'. It should be noted, however, that Smith does not argue that the other bases in terms of which individuals categorise each other are the 'real' ones. They too involve subjective participant's theories. It is therefore difficult to see why the fact that people do make subjective assessments of each other in terms of colour is left out of the sociologist's account.

We need not argue in this case, however, that there can never be any basis for distinguishing between the relative objectivity of assessment which actors make of each other in terms of colour, and those which they make in terms of reputation. All we do need to notice is that reputational and other social assessments

8. M. G. Smith, *The Plural Society in The British West Indies*, University of California Press, Berkeley, 1965, pp. 60–66.

are translated into a language of colour. Because of this we would say that the Caribbean situation was one which came within the purview of race relations studies. A man's position in this society is fixed in terms of a participant's theoretical argument that the colour of his skin is relevant.

This is, of course, by no means to say that there is not value in Smith's approach to Caribbean sociology in terms of a general theory of sociological pluralism. Such an approach we believe has great merits, if what we are seeking is an understanding of Caribbean society. If, however, our interest in studying this society is to throw greater light upon the sociological theory of race relations, then we must insist that this example is a relevant one.

The Caribbean case is a particularly difficult one. But its obverse is equally so. In the Caribbean case it is suggested men claim that they are classifying each other in terms of colour, when the actual basis on which they make their classifications is not one of colour at all. In some metropolitan societies on the other hand, where liberal ideologies prevent the open confession of colour prejudice and discrimination, men may claim that the discriminations and the classifications which they make have no reference to colour, whereas their practice shows that these classifications are colour-based. Here again, where our interpretation of the meaning of the actor's orientation to his fellows involves reference to colour, we are bound to consider this case as falling within the field of the sociology of race relations.

We do, therefore, wish to emphasise that the sociology of race relations must take account of subjective definitions, stereotypes, typifications and belief systems in the business of defining its field. And we would emphasise that patterns of social relations may be considerably changed through the causal agency of such belief systems. Yet at the same time we would also wish to emphasise the dependence of these belief systems on underlying structures. Thus, given that a true race relations situation exists when men have beliefs of a certain kind, it is also the case that such beliefs are associated only with a limited range of structures.

One of the tasks of the sociology of race relations therefore will be that of discovering and listing what these structures are.

Now, of course, as we have said, the very concept of social structures includes some reference to the concepts and expectations of participant actors. But it must now be said that some structures include such references more centrally than others. If we are talking about structures in which *alter's* compliance with *ego's* expectations is governed by norms, concepts play a rôle both in *ego's* classification of *alter*, and in applying moral rules to his behaviour towards *alter*. At the other extreme, where *ego* seeks to gain *alter's* compliance by coercion, however, no such normative element enters in. Between these two extremes one has the case in which *alter* complies because it is in his economic interest to do so. Here subjective factors are involved in *ego's* classification of *alter* and thereafter in terms of a restricted set of norms based upon economic rationality.

What is sometimes identified as the Marxist position is that which seeks to reduce all social structures to underlying economic forms, that is to say, seeks to reduce them to patterns of social relations in which *alter's behaviour*, (and for that matter *ego's*), is seen as being based upon the pursuit of his own economic interest. Not surprisingly it has been possible to demonstrate that many race relations situations cannot be explained in this way.

What is often forgotten in this dismissal of so-called Marxist theories, however, is that the economically non-rational aspects of behaviour might be due to a deviation not in the direction of normative compliance, but in the direction of compliance based upon coercion. Clearly such situations are likely to be common where conquest has occurred, and are a normal feature of colonial societies. In fact the most important direction in which a 'Marxist' approach has to be revised in the sociology of colonialism and race relations is in the direction suggested by Franz Oppenheimer.[9] Contrary to the Marxist view that social

9. F. Oppenheimer, *The State*, translation by G. M. Gitterman, Indianapolis, Ind., 1914.

differentiation is primarily to be explained in terms of the development of the social relations of production within a society, which is thought of as producing class conflict amongst a formerly united people, an alternative view, based upon the theories of Oppenheimer, might have much to offer the sociology of race relations. According to this view, intergroup relations have the form they do because the two groups involved were not originally one, but have been brought together into a single political framework as a result of the conquest by one of the other.

Thus, although we would not wish to deny that in almost every case of intergroup relations some subjective, conceptual and normative factor enters into the patterning of social relations, we would suggest that social relations in many colonial contexts tend in some degree towards the situation which would be represented by an ideal type of purely coercive compliance. In fact it is this feature of colonial societies, taken together with what we shall later define as racist theories, which defines the central kind of social situation with which we have to deal.

We are now somewhat nearer a position in which we will be able to take up the challenge presented to sociology by the biological experts. The biologists, it will be remembered, were simply called upon to pronounce upon the proper use of the concept 'race' in terms of the theory of their discipline. By so doing they might be said to have unmasked racism. The sociologist's task appears to involve unmasking in a more thorough-going sense. He has to show the way in which theories and ideas, falsely purporting to be based upon biological science, are built into the structure of social relationships. These theories and ideas are, however, not the only ones which might be built into such relationships, and the task of the sociologist might lie in exploring both the relationship between the racist theory and the underlying structure, and that between racist theories and other theories. The goal of research in this field would be to discover what kinds of theory were most likely to be associated with racism.

So far in this discussion we have assumed that it is always a feature of racist theory that it makes an appeal to biological science. Two qualifications of this position should therefore be made at this point. One is that, once we recognise that there may be some functional relationship between theories on the one hand and social structures on the other, the possibility arises that functional substitutes might be found when such theories are challenged. If this is the case it might be important to widen our range of interest and look, not merely at theories which have one particular content, but at all theories which fulfil a similar function. The other is that what we might call the conceptual content of social relations need not always be set out in the form of explicit and well-articulated theories. It may consist of nothing more than stereotypes, proverbs, symbols, folklore and so on, which, while it may be seen to have an internal logic of theoretical assumptions, does not at any point have these assumptions set out.

The difficulty which this point raises is that once we leave the clear and simple position that race relations problems exist where one or more of the parties to an intergroup encounter explain and justify the relationship between groups in terms of one single type of theory, which is at once recognisable by virtue of the fact that it appeals to biological theory, we appear to be in something of a morass. Are we to take it that any kind of theory may appear in a race relations situation, provided that a certain sort of structure of social relations is present?

Some sociologists would in fact take this step, but by so doing they virtually abolish the sociology of race relations as a special field. It becomes an indistinguishable part of a wider field such as the study of stratification. This is not the position which is taken here. What we wish to suggest is that limits can be set both to the kinds of theory and concepts and to the kind of structures which fall within the race relations field. These limits, however, should not narrowly confine us to the study of situations marked by the presence of explicitly biological theories. Nor should they lead to a diffusion of our interest to include, for example, all situations of social stratification. As a matter of convenience we will proceed by looking first at types of social structure which seem to be involved in race relations situations, rather than at theories. We do so, however, not because we have adopted the position that the theories are merely epiphenomenal, but because we think some kind of structural base is present in every race relations situation as a necessary if not as a sufficient element.

We may now proceed to a brief review of some of the theories which have been advanced as to the nature of the structural base of race relations problems by leading sociologists, before going on to make our own analysis in the chapters which follow. One group of these theories is focussed on the question of stratification, using that term in a fairly wide sense. The other draws attention to pluralism, i.e. the tendency of social systems to be divided, if not vertically, at least not simply into the sort of horizontal strata which the stratification theorists seem to imply.

Because of the fact that a sociological approach to race relations was first adopted in the United States much of the earliest theorising was devoted simply to the explanation of the relationships between whites and non-whites in that country. The most important subsequent argument has been about whether models derived from Europe could better explain the United States situation and about whether models developed in relation to American experience could adequately explain the kinds of structures which emerged in the Caribbean or Latin America or whether these societies were best explained in terms of a somewhat tentative framework developed in South East Asia. Thus much of the theorising to which we shall now refer has not been tested against the experience of African or Asian countries, nor even in relation to the experience of metropolitan European countries in dealing with coloured and non-coloured immigrant minorities.

The first American attempt at a theory of race relations and one which remains prominent even to the present day was W.

Lloyd Warner's theory of colour-caste.[10] According to this theory American society includes both class and caste divisions. The white population may be classified as belonging to one of a number of strata (or, as Warner would prefer to say, classes), which are arrived at by placing individuals in terms of two methods, which Warner elaborated in his studies of Yankee City. One of these classified the individuals according to their score on an index of objective and quantifiable status characteristics. The other was based upon the subjective assessments which individuals made of one another's status. Having elaborated this picture of the American stratification system Warner then went on to consider its relationship to the absorption of ethnic minorities. The Yankee City studies showed that most European minority groups moved up the stratification hierarchy over two or three generations, but that, so far as the negro population were concerned, however much they might achieve an improved position in terms of such objective status characteristics as income, they still found that there were barriers preventing their free association with whites at an equivalent level.

Warner suggested that the best way to conceptualise the relationship of the negroes to the stratification system was to begin by imagining that at the bottom of the stratification system there was a barrier far more impenetrable than those which divided the various strata or classes. When some of those beneath this barrier began to acquire characteristics which *prima facie* should have placed them higher up in the stratification system, the effect was not to breach the barrier but to tip it diagonally, so that there was the possibility of an individual negro becoming an upper-class negro, just as there was a possibility of a white becoming a poor white. There would, however, be less association between these two groups than there would between poor whites and middle-class whites or between upper class, middle-class and lower-class negroes.

10. W. Lloyd Warner, 'American Class and Caste', *American Journal of Sociology*, Vol. XLII, Sept. 1936, pp. 234–7.

Warner suggested that the barrier which thus split the stratification system into two was a caste barrier, at least in an incipient form, and he drew attention to similarities with the Hindu caste system, such as the taboos on intermarriage, eating together, and any other intimate form of association. Whether this fairly loose usage of the term caste is justified has been disputed, and probably the weight of opinion is against the introduction of the term caste to explain white-black relations in the United States. Nonetheless Warner's view that these relations cannot be explained in terms of normal stratification models survives, even if his notion of caste is rejected. Any adequate race relations theory must necessarily deal with this point.

O. C. Cox,[11] approaching the problem of the American negro from a sophisticated Marxist point of view, has sought to show that there are several crucial dissimilarities between intercaste and interracial relations as they occur in the United States, which make the use of the term caste in the latter case impermissible. He believes that a better theoretical construct for explaining race relations is that which may be derived from the Marxist theory of class conflict. Cox notes that the Hindu caste system is one in which there is a large measure of assent to the social inequalities and taboos on association amongst higher and lower castes, and that the central and characteristic feature of the system is the occupational specialisation of the castes. Neither of these two conditions prevails in the United States. The position of the negro worker in that society is that of the most exploited worker within a capitalist system of social relations of production. The absence of a race relations problem of the North American kind in Portuguese and Spanish Latin America is thus seen as explicable in terms of their being less advanced capitalist countries. So far from Catholic religion being a determining variable, its presence, like the absence of a race relations problem, is held to be dependent on the kind of economic system which exists.

Clearly the difficulty in sustaining Cox's theory is to show

11. O. C. Cox, *op. cit.*

why it is that white workers are not in the same position as negro workers. The simplest Marxist way out of this is simply to attribute the subjectively felt divisions within the working class to a state of 'false consciousness' fostered in its own interest by the bourgeoisie. A non-Marxist alternative would involve the introduction of a secondary hypothesis at this point. Thus it could be said that the position of the negro was explicable in terms of his relation to the means of production, but that a prior distinction had been made as to who should fill inferior working class rôles, and that this distinction was based upon non-economic criteria. As we shall argue later, this modified Marxist position does have considerable value in understanding the race relations situation not merely of the United States, but, even more, that of the Union of South Africa.

The most influential theory of social stratification in the United States today, that of Talcott Parsons, as set out in his 'Revised Analytic Approach to Social Stratification', treats the problem of ethnic differences as a factor which modifies the stratification system rather than as something which that system can explain. Thus like Warner, Parsons argues that 'in spite of the dispersion of members of given ethnic groups through the different levels of the main class structure, ethnicity to some degree tends to preserve relatively independent pyramids in the more general system'.[12]

Moreover, going beyond Warner, Parsons recognises that status within an ethnic group might be assigned on the basis of its own internal standards rather than those of the system as a whole and that 'the ethnic group, with regard both to its value patterns and to many other aspects of its status in the larger society, constitutes an entity somewhat apart, to which non-members react in patterned ways which in turn, help to determine the reactions of the members of the group'.[13]

These factors, which Parsons sees as being the consequence of

12. T. Parsons, *Essays in Sociological Theory*, Free Press, Glencoe, Ill., 1954, p. 424.
13. *Ibid.*, p. 425.

ethnicity, apply even more crucially in the narrower group of situations which we refer to as race relations situations. As we shall put it later on, neither pluralism of values nor the ascriptive allocation of rights in accordance with collectivity membership (i.e. discrimination) is a necessary consequence of systems of stratification envisaged in models like that of Parsons.

In American society Parsons has to admit that ethnicity provides an exception to the general pattern of stratification. But there clearly are a number of societies in which the fact of ethnic pluralism makes the application of the Parsonian type of stratification model quite impossible. This has been shown by M. G. Smith[14] in relation to the British West Indies and more recently by Tumin in a study of social stratification in Puerto Rico.[15]

What Parsons assumes is that all social systems have four major problems although different systems give priority to one rather than to the other. The four problems are represented in the older Parsonian language by the words *universalism, achievement, particularism* and *ascription*[16] and in the later language as *adaptation, goal attainment, integration* and *pattern maintenance,* and *tension management.*[17] In other and more comprehensible words a social system involves some rôles which are economic, technical or adaptive, some of which are directed towards ensuring that the system as a whole attains its end, some of which are concerned with preventing interests from clashing and thus holding the system together, and some of which are concerned with socialisation and social control. But societies at different stages of history and in different places have given differing priority to these rôles. It is characteristic of the American system that the most highly valued rôle is that which is concerned with adaptation, of the Soviet system that it gives

14. M. G. Smith, *op. cit.*, pp. 48–60.
15. M. M. Tumin and A. S. Feldman, *Social Class and Social Change in Puerto Rico*, Princeton University Press, Princeton, New Jersey, 1961.
16. T. Parsons, *The Social System*, Tavistock, London, 1952, p. 67.
17. T. Parsons, E. Shils, K. Naegele and J. Pitts, *Theories of Society*, Free Press, New York, 1965, pp. 30–79.

priority to goal-attainment, of pre-Nazi Germany that it emphasised the 'cultural ascriptive-qualitative focus', and of classical Chinese society that it emphasised integration. The problem of the stratification theorist is to find out what scale of priorities exist, and then to discover how the assignment of individuals to rôles, and of possessions to individuals, varies in accordance with this scale, both in the society at large, and within each institutional context. It is recognised that 'power' may lead to a deviation of the actual social pattern from that prescribed by the system of stratification values, but this does not alter the fact that such a system is an operative factor in that society.

The plain fact about many colonial societies however, is this: not merely is it the case that the actual distribution of rôles and rights deviates from the normal because of power, nor even that ethnicity leads to groups being assigned to positions collectively; there just *is* no common pattern. What one finds instead is that a number of groups have been brought together from different societies and that, even though there may be some point in saying that the value system of each gives priority to one or other of the sets of sub-system rôles, there is no shared value system on which an agreed pattern of stratification, either of all groups, or of all individuals within the society, could be based. The whole notion of a stratification system expressive of a consensually agreed value pattern appears to have significance solely within the constituent segments of society.

It does seem then that the various attempts which have been made to reduce the theory of race relations or of plural colonial societies to the position of being a particular case of stratification theory fail, although this is by no means to say that there are not some instances in which the structural base of a race relations situation is based upon some kind of stratification pattern. What has to be recognised is that such patterns are not the only ones involved, and, that taken by themselves, they cannot fully explain the variety of race relations situations with which we would wish to deal within a single frame of reference.

As against these attempts to reduce race relations theory to stratification theory we must now consider another influential tradition which reduces it to the theory of the plural society. According to this tradition, what we are concerned with in the study of race relations and of the plural society are neither hierarchically arranged castes, nor classes in conflict, nor a system of rôles arranged hierarchically according to their evaluation in terms of some set of ideal values. What we are concerned with are segments which cut across the strata, producing vertical rather than horizontal divisions within the society. This tradition takes as its starting point certain concepts derived from the work of J. S. Furnivall[18] and developed by a number of other writers of whom the most important and systematic is M. G. Smith.

Furnivall describes the main features of the plural society as follows:

> In Burma, as in Java, probably the first thing that strikes the visitor is the medley of peoples – European, Chinese, Indian and native. It is in the strictest sense a medley, for they mix but do not combine. Each group holds by its own religion, its own culture and language, its ideas and ways. As individuals they meet, but only in the market place, in buying and selling. There is a plural society, with different sections of the community living side by side, but separately within the same political unit. Even in the economic sphere there is a division of labour on racial lines.[19]

This is in fact a more complex statement than it appears to be at first sight. Most commonly Furnivall has been thought of as describing a state of affairs in which there is an almost total disjunction between the various ethnic groups. Real social life, according to this interpretation, is what goes on round the camp-fires of the separate communities when they are separated from one another. Their contact is a marginal business which takes place only in the market place and since this

18. J. S. Furnivall, *Netherlands, India*, Cambridge, 1939; *Colonial Policy and Practice*, Cambridge, 1948; M. G. Smith, *op. cit.*, pp. 66–91.
19. J. S. Furnivall, *Colonial Policy and Practice*, p. 304.

produces no common will, no normative order, is of little interest to the sociologist.

In fact Furnivall specifically mentions three types of social bond in the passage quoted. He speaks of the 'religion, culture and language, ideas and ways' of the separate groups, referring apparently to normatively bound social relations. But he also speaks of a single 'political unit' thus recognising coercive ties and of 'a division of labour on racial lines' recognising utilitarian and economic bonds.

Smith reads Furnivall as arguing that the 'plural economy' of South East Asia rests upon an underlying social pluralism. He himself prefers to 'take the argument back one step further' and to look at what to him as an anthropologist is the most fundamental thing of all, namely cultural pluralism. The core of any culture is its 'institutional system' and what characterises a plural society is that its different segments have different institutional systems. Such institutional systems include 'kinship, education, religion, property and economy, recreation and certain sodalities'.[20] It does not, however, include government because without a single governmental institution we should not have a society at all. We should have several coexisting societies. But Smith goes further than merely saying that there should be a shared governmental institution. He argues that, 'Given the fundamental differences of belief, value and organisation that connote pluralism, the monopoly of power by one cultural section is the essential precondition for the maintenance of the total society in its current form.'[21]

Pluralism in a society is not to be confused with stratification. The relationship between the two structural principles is described by Smith as follows:

Within each cultural section of a plural society we may expect to find some differences of stratification or social class. These cultural sections themselves are usually ranked in a hierarchy, but the hierarchic arrangement of the sections differs profoundly in its basis

20. M. G. Smith, *op. cit.*, p. 82.
21. *Ibid.*, p. 86.

and character from the hierarchic organisation within each severally. The distribution of status within each cultural section rests on common values and criteria quite specific to that group, and this medley of sectional value systems rules out the value consensus that is the prerequisite for any status continuum. Thus the plurality is a discontinuous status order lacking any foundation in a system of common interests and values, while its component sections are genuine status continua, distinguished by their differing systems of value action and social relations.[22]

But later he goes even further in emphasising the absence of a normative order uniting the sections: 'There is no inherent reason why all cultural sections in a plural society should be ranked hierarchically'.[23]

But if the study of plural societies cannot be reduced to the study of social stratification, neither can it, according to Smith, be reduced to the study of race relations:

To do so is to mistake the social myth for reality, and thus to miss the structure that underlies it and gives it both force and form. . . . It often happens that racially distinct groups form a common homogeneous society, as for instance among the Hausa-Fulani of Northern Nigeria. Conversely, we sometimes find culturally distinct groups that belong to the same racial stock expressing their differences in racial terms.[24]

In view of what was said at the beginning of this chapter about the notion of 'racial stocks', one may well be surprised at the uncritical use of this term by Smith. Probably, however, he does have quite definite classifications made by physicalist anthropologists in mind when he uses the term here. Usually, however, he is simply trying to make the point that those who emphasise race relations as the basis for the study of plural societies are referring primarily to colour differences. Against such writers he argues as we have seen that colour, as it is subjectively understood, often means social and cultural colour.

22. *Ibid.*, p. 28.
23. *Ibid.*, p. 83.
24. *Ibid.*, p. 89.

For our part we do not intend to 'mistake the social myth for the reality' in this book. What we should say, however, is that so far as we are concerned the social myth is part of the reality. What we envisage is a situation in which two distinct groups are held together within a single political framework, in which there is an unequal apportionment of rights between these groups, and in which, finally, the system is justified by appeal to some kind of deterministic theory such as a racial one. It is this approach which will enable us to bring together in a single frame of reference the study, not merely of the Caribbean societies with which Smith is especially concerned, but of a far more diverse range of situations resulting from colonial conquest and pluralism.

One further theoretical point which arises from Smith's dismissal of a race relations approach might also be noted here. In his account of the plural society he had insisted on the looseness of the relationship between the segments, arguing that they were bound together through political domination by one of them rather than through any kind of overall consensus as to the qualities meriting higher or lower prestige. What is suggested in his attempt to eliminate colour differences from the discussion, however, is that there *is* some kind of status continuum which stretches at least from the ex-slave negro group through coloured groups to the white West Indians at the apex of the status pyramid.

Finally Smith has some difficulty in distinguishing between the cultural diversity which commonly occurs in advanced societies which contain cultural minorities, and the cultural pluralism of plural societies. He meets this difficulty by suggesting a distinction between 'incompatible institutional forms' which is the case in a plural society and 'stylistic variations'.[25] This distinction remains somewhat unclear.

It is perhaps interesting that although Smith leans very heavily upon Malinowski's definitions of 'culture' and 'institution', as expounded in his 'Scientific Theory of Culture',[26]

25. *Ibid.*, p. 83.
26. B. Malinowski, *A Scientific Theory of Culture*, University of N. Carolina Press, Chapel Hill, 1944.

he does not apparently pay much attention to 'The Dynamics of Culture Change',[27] in which one might say Malinowski set out his ideas on the plural society in Africa. In sharp contrast to Smith, Malinowski suggests that, in listing the institutions in the plural society, one should not merely list those of each of its component sections, but should add a 'third column' to include institutions which arise within the process of culture contact. Such an institution according to Malinowski is the system of compound labour, found within South African society, but having no parallel either in English or Dutch society on the one hand, or in African societies on the other.

The institutions which relate to the employment of labour in any society differ in the degree to which they depend upon normative, utilitarian or coercive sanctions, but, whatever our interpretation of slavery or of compound labour in South Africa, it must surely be agreed that these are institutions of the whole society and not simply of one cultural or social segment. It is only because of the restricted range of interest dictated by his anthropologist's approach that Smith is able to include forms of 'property and economy' in his institutional sets which are said to pertain to the separate segments.

What one would have to do to amend Smith's theory at this point is to recognise that the segments are bound together economically as well as politically. It is true, of course, that in plural societies the social relations of production involve an element of coercion, which might justify their assimilation under the heading of the political system. Smith, however, makes things worse for himself by suggesting that the authority system of slavery has to be understood as part of a larger class of culturally dictated norms. He may be right in this and we shall, in a later chapter discuss the degree to which slavery is affected by social norms. The point here is simply that the institution which Smith describes clearly straddles the segments.

Like stratification theorists, Smith is a reductionist when it

27. B. Malinowski, *The Dynamics of Culture Change*, Yale University Press, 1945.

comes to the study of 'race relations' (meaning in this case
relations between groups who see each other as having clear
differences of physical characteristics such as skin colour). We
should at least note before passing on that one recent writer
Hoetink[28] has opposed even Smith's form of reductionism. He
suggests that part of the stock of cultural ideals possessed by any
ethnic group or segment is a certain 'somatic norm image', that
is to say, a certain conception of the kinds of human being who
are regarded either as beautiful, acceptable or as belonging to
one's own group. It should, however, be noted that Hoetink
doesn't claim that such distinctions have some objective validity.
He sees them as a cultural variable. In saying ourselves that the
myth is part of the reality we wish to include such a perspective.
Apart from explicit racist theories, such factors as 'somatic
norm images' certainly form part of the ideological content of
intergroup relations.

It is important to notice that Furnivall and Smith alike see the
political order or political domination as of the essence of plural
society situations. We only underline this when we say that
coercive economic institutions are a characteristic feature of such
situations. We should now note that there is one final group of
theories relevant to the study of race relations which gives some
priority to the notion of conquest, coercion and political
domination. This is the set of theories which discusses not
stratification or pluralism, but 'minorities'. Such theories are
wider in scope than the field of race relations studies, but as the
basic definitions of minority studies show, they certainly include
the study of racial, colonial and plural situations as well as
having the advantage from our point of view of drawing
attention to the sort of racial situations which occur in advanced
metropolitan countries.

Louis Wirth has defined a minority as a group of people who
because of their physical or cultural characteristics, are singled out
from others in the society in which they live for differential and un-

28. H. Hoetink, *The Two Variants in Carribean Race Relations*, Institute of
Race Relations, Oxford University Press, 1967, especially pp. 120 ff.

equal treatment, and who therefore regard themselves as objects of collective discrimination. The existence of a minority in a society implies the existence of a corresponding dominant group with higher social status and greater privileges. Minority status carries with it the exclusion from full participation in the life of the society.[29]

What is referred to here is not necessarily a group which is in a numerical minority, but a group which is in an inferior political position. By this definition it is the numerical African majority in South Africa who are the minority in that country, not the ruling white group. Equally even in non-settler societies and colonies the political subordination of the native people would make them a minority.

Actually neither Wirth, nor Simpson and Yinger,[30] who quote him, would in fact wish to go this far. Clearly it makes nonsense of the concept to call the Indian people during the period of the British Empire a minority in their own country. But there is some advantage in speaking of negro and East Indian minorities in British Guiana under colonial rule and thereby posing the question as to whether there is not something sociologically similar between their condition and that of, say, the American negroes, Polish immigrants in America, or the Basque people in contemporary Spain.

Wagley and Harris[31] come nearest to a precise definition of minorities which is nonetheless wide enough to cover the necessary ground when they say that

(1) minorities are subordinate segments of complex state societies; (2) minorities have special physical or cultural traits which are held in low esteem by dominant segments of the society; (3) minorities are self-conscious units bound together by the special traits which their members share and by the special disabilities which these bring; (4) membership in a minority is transmitted by a rule of descent which is

29. L. Wirth, in R. Linton (ed.), *The Science of Man in the World Crisis*, Columbia University Press, New York, 1945, p. 347.

30. G. E. Simpson and J. M. Yinger, *Racial and Cultural Minorities*, Harper and Row, New York, 1965.

31. C. Wagley and M. Harris, *Minorities in the New World*, Columbia University Press, New York, 1964.

capable of affiliating succeeding generations even in the absence of readily apparent special cultural or physical traits; (5) minority peoples, by choice or necessity, tend to marry within the group.[32]

As in Smith's use of the concept 'plural society', so here we find that Wagley and Harris place emphasis upon the importance of a coercive political institution as the precondition of minority problems. 'Only with the development of the state', they write,

did human societies become equipped with a form of social organisation which could bind masses of culturally and physically heterogeneous strangers into a single social entity . . . as primitive peoples derive their cohesion largely from a common culture and from kinship and other kinds of personal ties, state societies are held together largely by the existence of a central political authority which claims a monopoly of coercive power over all persons within a given territory. Theoretically with a sufficiently strong development of the apparatus of government, a state society can extend law and order over limitless subgroups of strangers who neither speak the same language, worship the same gods, nor strive for the same values.

Yet the growth of the state form of organisation did not entirely replace the principles by which unity is achieved among primitive peoples.[33]

In fact it is not the case, as Hobhouse[34] once hopefully suggested, that societies based upon citizenship come to replace those based upon kinship. Rather the political principle is one which operates in the creation of a plural unit whereas the kin and, one might say, culture principle operates within each group. It should be clear, in fact, that Wagley and Harris' account of the nature of minority situations is very close to that which Smith gives of the plural society.

There are circumstances in which a minority seeks its own disappearance through assimilation within the cultural and social system of the group which dominates the state. There are

32. *Ibid.*, p. 10.
33. *Ibid.*, p. 242.
34. L. T. Hobhouse, *Morals in Evolution*, Chapman Hall, London, 1950.

also circumstances in which the group seeks simply to coexist, maintaining its own culture and social system along with that of the dominant group. In either case it may occur that the dominant group takes account of and grants the minority's wishes. In so far as this happens such a minority would cease to be of interest to us, seeking as we are to define the limits, not of minority group studies, but of race relations. We will suggest that some element of conflict between groups, and of coercion of one group by another, is an essential part of the structural base of a race relations situation.

Most commonly, however, whether the minority seeks to assimilate, to coexist, to secede or to reverse the existing order of things by becoming the dominant group, its wishes are not acceded to. In some measure it suffers unfavourable discrimination. When this is the case we are dealing with a situation in which a race relations problem may emerge.

In fact an extremely important variable in minority group studies is, as Simpson and Yinger point out, that which relates to the policy pursued by the dominant group towards a minority. There are at least six possible policies including a number of sub-variants which Simpson and Yinger list as follows:

1. Assimilation:
    (*a*) Forced;
    (*b*) Permitted.
2. Pluralism.
3. Legal protection of minorities.
4. Population transfer:
    (*a*) Peaceful transfer;
    (*b*) Forced migration.
5. Continued subjugation.
6. Extermination.[35]

Certainly, where policies 1(*a*), 4(*b*), 5 or 6 hold, we have the basis of a race relations problem. We assume that 5 is the forced

35. Simpson and Yinger, *op. cit.*, p. 20.

version of 2. So far as legal protection of minorities is concerned, this is often an oblique indication of a race relations problem, in that it assumes that there is a group which is seeking to exercise power, albeit illegal power, against the minority.

In their study of minorities in the Western Hemisphere Wagley and Harris point out that the case studies which they made were all of vanquished enemies, outright slaves or poor immigrants.[36] If we were to add to this the case of refugee immigrant minorities who might not be poor, and indentured labourers and trading minorities who move in under the protection of a political conqueror, we should probably have an exhaustive list of the kinds of minority groups, who might become party to a race relations situation. Thus we could give examples of the various types as follows:

(1) Vanquished enemies: the American Indians, the Africans in South Africa, the French in Canada, the Afrikaners in South Africa.

(2) Outright slaves: West African negroes in British territories and East African peoples enslaved by Arab societies.

(3) Poor immigrants: Italian, Polish and many other minorities in the United States; West Indian, Pakistani or Indian immigrants in Britain.

(4) Political refugees: Jewish refugees from Nazism, Hungarian and other refugees from the communist world.

(5) Indentured labourers: Indian and Chinese workers in various British colonial territories.

(6) Trading minorities: Jewish, Muslim Indian and Chinese traders in various parts of Africa, Asia and Europe.

Whether or not these minority situations become the bases of race relations situations depends, both on the policy of the politically dominant group on whose authority they live, and, if they suffer unfavourable discrimination, on the kind of justification given for that discrimination.

36. Wagley and Harris, op. cit., p. 265.

Harris[37] has raised the very important question of the relationship between minorities, classes and castes. So far as the relationship to class is concerned, what we said earlier about stratification theories may suffice. But there are some aspects of the situation of certain kinds of minority group which are suggestive of caste and these are worth looking at.

There do appear to be in most societies certain occupations and tasks, which are thought to be either incompatible with the values of, or beneath the dignity of, the dominant group, and indeed of some minorities. In these cases an outside group may be informally licensed to perform the necessary task and criticised, abused, blamed and punished for doing it. This is true both of certain trading rôles and of menial work of particular kinds. Jews in Europe, Indians, Syrians and Lebanese in Africa become involved in the societies to which they emigrate in the first capacity. Coloured workers undertaking tasks of an arduous and dirty kind in England, when no other workers can be found to undertake them, provide an example of the second. The term 'pariah' has been used for both such groups, and the usage of this term raises the question of whether it would be right to envisage certain kinds of plural societies, in which there was an occupational specialisation of minorities together with the recognition of certain outcaste or pariah rôles as caste societies. Our own view would be that this would overstate what is nothing more than a tendency. Nonetheless the main point about pariah rôles playing an important part in minority-group situations, and in plural societies, stands.

Related to this is another point. This is that, apart from being discriminated against and performing unwanted tasks, some minority groups might be singled out as scapegoats by the dominant group. Such a contingency is always possible in a changing society which seeks to maintain the position of a dominant group even in times of crisis. This possibility, more-

37. M. Harris, 'Caste, Class and Minority', *Social Forces*, March 1959, pp. 248–254.

over, is of some importance to us, since it is one which frequently leads to racist justifications and theories.

From this review of some of the basic sociological theories about the kinds of societies in which race relations situations and problems occur, we may now define our own approach to the problem of defining the sociological field of race relations. It includes the following three elements:

(1) a situation of differentiation, inequality and pluralism as between groups;

(2) the possibility of clearly distinguishing between such groups by their physical appearance, their culture or occasionally merely by their ancestry;

(3) the justification and explanation of this discrimination in terms of some kind of implicit or explicit theory, frequently but not always of a biological kind.

Broadly speaking we shall be referring to each of these topics in turn in subsequent chapters. But it is not easy to separate theories and discriminatory practice from our account of structure, so that it is desirable to treat this aspect of the question more extensively than the others.

The logic of our plan of study emerges from the related studies we have reviewed. From Warner, Parsons and Smith we see that there is a kind of discrimination against *groups* involved which does not coincide with more normal stratification patterns. From Cox, Furnivall, Smith, Wagley and Harris, we learn that there is an element of coercion involved in the constitution of the societies with which we are concerned. From all of the writers we learn that a pattern of intergroup relations marked by intergroup coercion and discrimination, might exist, which is explicable independently of any notion of racial differences between the participant groups. But, given that this is the case, we have to look at those cases in which differences, which may exist for other reasons, are rationalised and justified in terms of race.

So far as the basic structures are concerned the organisation of this study is affected by its critical orientation to many of the studies we have discussed. As we see it, political and economic coercion is a central theme within the kinds of society we shall be discussing. It is not therefore profitable to talk about societies in general, about their value systems and their stratification systems, unless we look first at the institutions around which the larger social order is built. Before we go on then to talk about the stratification of plural societies, it is necessary that we should look at the basic political and economic institutions of colonialism.

On the other hand, precisely because we place so much emphasis upon colonialism, it is desirable that we should go on after these two chapters to look at the problem of race relations as it occurs, not in colonial, but in metropolitan societies. Our previous review of some of the issues involved in the sociology of colonialism will be illuminating at this point, but it will also be necessary to take account of other kinds of minorities apart from colonial immigrants along the lines suggested by Wagley and Harris, and Simpson and Yinger. The third of our structural chapters, therefore, will be entitled 'Minorities in Metropolitan Society'.

2. The Social Institutions of Colonialism: Conquest and Unfree Labour

Our approach to the study of the social structures which underly race relations situations differs from that of most of the studies which we reviewed in the previous chapter in two major respects. One is that we take the view that, before going on to talk about the structure of society in general, it is important to look at the social relations which characterise the society's productive institutions, since these contribute important meanings to the overall social pattern. The other is that we draw attention to the fact that the social relations of production, as well as the larger social structure, are based upon the coercion of one group by another, a state of affairs which is most likely to come about in conditions where one group on a lower technological level than another is conquered by the other.

So far as the first of these points is concerned, we go further than most critics of stratification theories. Many of them have drawn attention to the absence of a value consensus as the differentiating feature of the societies with which we have to deal. But, because concentration is on the social system as a whole, it is difficult to see what binds it together and makes it a system. We suggest that, in so far as there is no binding normative order social organisation, compliance must either be based upon political or economic factors, that is to say, on the use of force or on the appeal to economic self-interest. A good point at which to start the analysis of these basic social bonds is at the point of production, where one group of men put their labour at the disposal of another.

With this said, it is necessary to add immediately that the distinction between economic and political orders, and between coercive and utilitarian sanctions, is very difficult to maintain outside the context of advanced capitalist countries. In fact it would appear that the application of the market mechanism as a means of arranging relations between employers and employees is, in any long historical perspective, somewhat unusual. Mostly men work for themselves and their kin or they work for others because they have been forced to. Once they are so forced, it is true, they may come to, or be trained to, a subjective belief that the authority of their masters is legitimate. But, in any case, we have to recognise here the structural importance, not simply of political authority or market forces, but of that wider factor to which Weber refers and which Parsons translates as 'imperative co-ordination' and Bendix simply as 'domination'.[1]

Unlike many other sociologists of his time, Weber[2] saw the fact of free labour and, more widely, the orientation of capitalist enterprise to the exploitation of peaceful market opportunities, as a historically unique achievement in West European society. Free labour was to be contrasted with a variety of other forms, while capitalism most normally took the form of adventurer or booty capitalism. The essence of these 'economic' institutions therefore seemed to lie, except in the case of Northwest European and American capitalism, in the use of force.

Marxist thought, based as it is upon the analysis, albeit in a new and radical way, of the laws of the capitalist market, has done much to direct attention away from these factors. Social differentiation for Marx arose perhaps, in the first instance from the unscrupulousness of individuals taking advantage of their control of important economic resources to reduce others to subjection, but the basic reason for inequality and for the class struggle is the development of power in market situations. This

1. T. Parsons, *The Theory of Social and Economic Organisation*, Free Press, Glencoe, Ill., 1964, Chapter 3; R. Bendix, *Max Weber, An Intellectual Portrait*, Heinemann, London, 1960, Part 3.

2. M. Weber, *Economy and Society*, Bedminster Press, New York, 1968, Vol. I, Chapter 2; *General Economic History*, Collier Books, New York, 1961.

was the most important of a number of Marxist theses disputed by Franz Oppenheimer.[3]

Oppenheimer argued that the injustice even of the urban workers' situation could be traced back to unjust rural institutions and to the existence of a class of large landed proprietors. Whether or not the economic and sociological arguments which he presents actually justify this view, he did offer an important corrective to Marxism in showing that European economic institutions had developed consequentially from Roman imperialism, from the conquest of one barbarian tribe by another, and from the barbarian conquest of the Roman empire. The additional importance of Oppenheimer's work however, lies, as does so much of the comparative and historical sociology of Max Weber, in its applicability to the constitution of new forms of society on a pluralistic basis as the result of European expansion and European conquest in Asia, Africa and the Americas. In the new societies which were formed, the historical processes which Oppenheimer was able to see dimly reflected in European institutions, and the structures which Weber described in order to point out the contrast between occidental capitalism and other social forms, were the processes and structures which were central to any serious sociological analysis.

Smith, it will be remembered, insists that if a plural society is to be a society at all, there must be a monopoly of political power in the hands of one of the segments. This is a tenable position so long as what one is seeking to do is to make comparative and relatively speaking static studies of plural societies. If, however, one is interested in the question of how these societies came into being, and if one is interested, not in plural societies, but in race relations, then this limitation cannot be maintained. In order fully to understand the element of force and violence involved in intergroup relations, one has to see the groups at a stage when there is still some degree of open conflict between them.

3. Oppenheimer, *op. cit.*

We need not press the point here that any international conflict may be thought of in racist terms, and may be included within the total field of race relations studies. What is more important, however, is the frontier situation in which two groups with unequal technological and educational standards confront each other but the superior group has not yet imposed its rule on the inferior one. Such was the situation when the barbarians were at the gates of the Roman empire, and such was the situation as between settlers and natives on the Eastern Cape frontier in South Africa. Toynbee[4] has used the term external proletariat to describe the position of the barbarian tribes, and Roux[5] has applied the term in the South African case. It is a useful term, in so far as it emphasises that the inferior group is already caught up within the social system of the superior group, and that its own institutional system is not viable, even though it retains formal independence.

One possible outcome of this situation of course, is that the barbarians might have the military means to conquer their 'civilised' neighbours, but if they really are an external proletariat they likely to be culturally changed in the process of taking over the superior civilisation. More frequently the barbarians are defeated, and will be incorporated in the civilised society only on its own terms. In this case the possibility of discrimination and of racist theory arises.

The interesting thing about such frontier situations is that an ideological debate ensues about the terms on which the 'barbarians' are to be included in the civilised society. This debate is especially acute, because settlers on the colonial frontiers of the early eighteenth century were often imbued with the political ideas of the French Revolution, so far as the structure of their own group was concerned. When outsiders were incorporated, they either had to be included as free and equal fellow-citizens, or it had to be argued that there were certain kinds of men who were non-men in that the revolutionary ideals did not apply to

4. A. Toynbee, *A Study of History*, New York, 1934.
5. E. Roux, *Time Longer than Rope*, Gollancz, London, 1949.

them. Thus it was possible for a French settler in Haiti to support the revolution in France and yet oppose the uprising of the slaves of Haiti. And in South Africa some twenty-five years later the missionary Dr Philip might plead for equal treatment for African and coloured citizens before the law, while the farmers were insisting upon their rights to prevent the free movement of African labour and upon the unfettered right to punish farm-servants as they saw fit.[6]

A frontier situation of this kind, of course, comes to an end when a conquered people are incorporated by another society. Rarely is it the case, however, that they are incorporated on terms of absolute equality. From the start there is a distinction far more fundamental than any class distinction between the conquerors and the conquered. And, if the conquered retain any visible sign such as their own distinctive physical characteristics or distinct cultural practices, there will be no possibility of mobility from one group to another. Moreover, even when there is no such external sign, there is still the possibility that affiliation by descent might still be recognised, as Wagley and Harris pointed out in the passage which we quoted in the last chapter.

In circumstances like these, one feature of the intergroup tension which should be noted is that psychologically speaking and in terms of the implicit meanings of the language which is used in the society, thinking about the other group means thinking about a situation of war. This is even more likely to be the case if, after successful pacification for a time, the conquered group attempts to revolt. Thus the Mau-Mau rebellion in Kenya reproduced for the white settlers something of the experience of the frontier, even though those whom they were fighting and whom they feared were the citizens of their own country.

So far, of course, what we have been assuming is the sort of situation in which a gradually expanding settlement by settler farmers from one of the advanced countries moves gradually into conflict with native peoples. This was the situation in settler

6. W. M. Macmillan, *Bantu, Boer and Briton*, Oxford, 1963.

Africa as it was in the United States of America. It is, however, by no means the only pattern of conquest.

Weber points out that most usually colonialism involves a kind of fiscal operation.[7] The military power of a subordinate nation is broken and its own head is required to see to it that some form of tribute is regularly delivered. In return for this he receives some kind of feudal protection. Alternatively the right to gather in the tribute might be sold to tax-farming capitalist enterprises. Indirect rule represented the first of these alternatives in the British Empire, while the exploitation of colonial territories through chartered companies represented the second.

The conquest of large parts of Central and South America by the Spanish *conquistadores* involves a more direct approach to the business of getting the wealth of the conquered into the hands of the conquerors. Even there, however, the simple plunder of the earliest years soon gave way to the creation of more formal institutions of production and labour exploitation.

The social system set up by the European colonising powers in the new societies in their colonial territories was in some cases feudal, and in some cases capitalistic. The distinction between the two types is a matter to which we shall have to return. For the moment, however, we should notice that, whether it is a feudal or a capitalistic order which is established, there are usually some native people who are left out of full participation within it. This is the situation of the peasant in the subsistence sector of the colonial economy, and it is the situation of those people who are left to live a 'protected' minority existence on reservations.

Whether this subsistence island within the colonial economy represents a privilege, a special form of exploitation, or merely the fact that the economy has more resources than it can use, may vary with different societies and different points in history. Clearly there are some instances in which the colonial powers are anxious to get farmers to move into cash crop production or out of farming into urban industrial work. There are other

7. M. Weber, *Economy and Society*, Vol. II, Chapter 9, pp. 913–21.

cases in which they have sought to hold back this movement to the annoyance of modernising elements in the native population. And whereas, whichever course they adopted, they might sometimes have done it for the welfare of what appeared a backward element in the population, they might also have done it in order to step up the level of exploitation. Whatever they do, however, an important dimension of social differentiation in colonial society is between those who fully participate in the new economy and those who exist outside of it.

The colonial enterprise involves in the first place the capture of land and other physical resources. One possibility after this has occurred is the development of an estate system in which new owners either develop the land in the form of large estates which they either work themselves in such non-labour-intensive activities as sheep-rearing, or let out in smaller lots to tenant farmers. More commonly, however, the possession of the land by itself is not enough. Those who have been expelled from the land have to be compelled by one means or another to work for the new proprietor.

The new proprietor may set up a self-sufficient manorial unit in which the object of the exercise is production for the master's table and household, or he may set up an agricultural unit which is oriented to production for the market, that is to say, the manor might develop into a plantation. The basic economic units of the North, Central and Latin American colonies lay somewhere between these two types.

Whether the productive unit is organised for the purpose of producing subsistence or of producing for the market, and whether, for that matter, it is an agricultural, mining, industrial, or merely a domestic enterprise, there are a number of different ways in which the problem of providing a labour supply might be dealt with. In the American colonies established by the English, the Spanish, the Portuguese, the French and the Dutch, the characteristic way of dealing with the problem in the long run was through the revival on a large scale of the institution of slavery. But before this solution was widely accepted, as well as contemporaneously with the practice of slavery, a number of other types of labour systems were tried.

In the Spanish colonies the basic institution for the organisation of labour was the *encomienda*. One of its early critics refers to it as follows:

> The greatest evil which has caused the total destruction of these lands and which will continue unless a remedy be found and which is neither just nor can it be or ought it be allowed in reason is the *encomienda* of Indians as it now exists, that is to say, being allotted for life in order that working as they are worked, all profit deriving from their work goes to those who hold them in *encomienda* . . .[8]

The moral denunciation apart, what seems to be suggested here is a feudal institution, at least in the sense that men are required to give labour services in return for protection. But it needs to be distinguished sharply from both serfdom on a manor and from slavery. The *encomendero* did not, like the mediaeval lord of the manor, own the land which his Indians might work. And on the other hand the Indians were not condemned to perpetual and hereditary servitude. According to Wagley and Harris the *encomienda* was essentially a kind of tax-farming in which the tax or tribute was for some time paid in the form of labour service. As they describe it

> a Spanish colonist was granted the right to collect tribute from the Indians of a given area. The right was limited to one or two generations and it did not include ownership of the land on which the Indian lived. The *encomendero* might collect tribute in food or personal services. Thus many mines were operated by workers paying off tribute and, for a time the *encomendero* could hire out his serfs to work for others. But by the middle of the sixteenth century it was decreed that tribute might not be paid in personal labour but only in goods and money.[9]

It would, therefore, seem that the *encomienda* in its pure form

8. L. Hanke, *The Spanish Struggle for Justice in the Conquest of America*, The University of Pennsylvania Press, Philadelphia, 1949, p. 86.
9. Wagley and Harris, *op. cit.*, p. 53.

was a temporary phenomenon, which belonged to the initial period of Spanish colonialism, when the primary problem was to find labour for specific tasks not necessarily connected with agriculture, as slavery so often was, and quite often connected with mining. But this is by no means to say that it was not characterised by coercion of the most violent sort. During the sixteenth century it should be noted the population of the various kingdoms in what is now called Mexico were reduced by about 50%. It is against the background of a death rate of this kind that loyal submission to a master within an institutional framework such as that of the *encomienda* becomes possible.

When the *encomienda* ceased to operate as a forced labour institution, it was replaced by *repartimiento*, a system under which Indians could be called upon to do work which was in the public interest. But settlers quickly came to apply their own liberal interpretation to the term 'public interest'. Under this system a percentage of the Indian population could be called upon at the will of the government to work for wages in mines, on plantations, or in public works.

Finally, the system which the Spaniards adopted for recruiting Indians into the labour force was that of debt-peonage. Under this system the peon became indebted through being granted a piece of land or an advance of wages in return for labour services. This system was apparently deliberately used in the sense that settlers would set out to put Indians into debt in order to force them to work.

Some of the institutions which we have just discussed are repeated in Africa at a later period and in slightly modified forms. Before we turn to them, however, it is necessary that we should look at the development of labour institutions in English and Portuguese America, particularly with regard to the development of the slave plantation and related social forms.

The first negroes to be introduced into the United States in 1619 were not legally defined as slaves in the complete sense in which the status of slavery eventually came to be defined. According to Elkins,

It was apparently possible for the earliest negroes to fall into various servant categories long familiar to the common law of England, none of which in a practical sense included perpetual and inherited chattel bondage. The bulk of agricultural labourers coming into the colonies at this period were white servants whose terms as time went on were to become more and more definitely fixed by indenture and the 'Negroes' so far as the law was concerned could be regarded as servants like the rest; there was no articulated legal structure in the colonies to impede their becoming free after a term of service and entering society as artisans and holders of property. Indeed it was still assumed that the profession of Christianity should still make a difference in status. Manumission, moreover, for whatever reason, was a practice common enough to be taken for granted and was attended by no special legal restrictions.[10]

As we shall see in a moment, Portuguese and Spanish law did recognise the institution of slavery from the outset, although in such a way as to place far more severe formal restrictions on the slaveowner than in the American pattern, but, the comparison of the English and Spanish institutions apart, what is interesting in the above quotation from Elkins is that it shows how many degrees and gradations of unfree labour there are before one reaches the extreme state of the rightlessness of labour exhibited in North American slavery.

On the other hand, terms like 'indentured labour', 'contract labour' and 'indentured servants', are used with little precision and cover a great many different cases. Englishmen who employed other Englishmen as servants would impose fairly lenient contractual terms on them, even though the servant might have been forced into indentures through indebtedness, through unemployment, through being a prisoner of war (as in the case of English Civil War prisoners), or through being simply a convicted criminal. Indian indentured workers recruited to work on sugar plantations after emancipation again might be severely exploited as workers and have severe restrictions placed on their freedom during the period of their indentures, but could look

10. S. M. Elkins, *Slavery*, The Universal Library, Grosset and Dunlap, New York, 1963, p. 38.

forward to an eventual period of freedom. On the other hand, there have been cases in which the recruitment of contract labour particularly among negro peoples has been very similar at the point of recruitment to the capture or purchase of slave labour. Obviously a great deal depends on the amount of force which can be deployed by the original recruiting agent. If the contract labourer really has no alternative but to sign on then his contract will be as harsh and exploitative as minimum government standards allow. Thereafter, the only thing which can make a difference is the relative benevolence of the employer and the government concerned. There are some variations in this respect, but they are hardly as significant as those which arise from differences in the amount of coercion which can be employed in the recruiting situation.

This discussion is, of course, relevant to the question of how the various ethnic strata of segments in a plural society come to be accorded the varying degrees of prestige which they do. What we would suggest is that the relevant difference between various groups is not simply one of differences of cultural practice, nor yet the possession of qualities relevant to the attainment of the system's functional ends. What differentiates the various groups is the degree of violence to which they or their ancestors have been subjected, and hence the degree to which the segment as a whole has, as part of its cultural tradition, a tradition of freedom. Hence the low status of the negro in any system of racial or ethnic stratification in a plural society has much to do with the fact that he comes from a people who were more unfree than any others.

Our aim in this book is to outline a typology of race relations structures, and it is not therefore our aim to go into vivid detail with regard to the history of slavery. Nonetheless, it is essential to draw attention at the outset of our discussion of the institution to the extremity of the violence which was used in the recruitment of slave labour for the American colonies.

Elkins[11] suggests that there were six shocks involved in the

11. Elkins, *op. cit.*, pp. 98–103.

business of being captured and sold into slavery for the African negro. There was the shock of capture, the shock of the march to the sea, the shock of being sold, the shock of the Middle Passage, the shock of resale to an employer, and finally the shock of the seasoning period. But the notion of shock refers only to the survivors, and, underlying all these six shocks, is the simplest one of all, namely the shock that two thirds of those in a similar position died before actually becoming slaves. Little wonder then that Elkins has to grope to find any kind of historical equivalent. The nearest he can find is in the experience of concentration camp inmates in Nazi Germany. What happened to them is, of course, relevant to the study of race relations and we shall return to this question later. But, in order to put the fact of slavery into its proper perspective, it is necessary to recognise that in many respects the shock of enslavement was some hundreds of times more brutal than that of the concentration camp inmates. We suggest indeed that the violence used by those who ran the slave trade is the most important underlying fact in the structure of race relations situations even when what we are studying is a society in which emancipation has long since been carried through.

Perhaps, indeed, it is the fact of enslavement rather than anything which happens during the operation of slave plantations which is most important to the emergence of subsequent race relations patterns. For, in being recruited as a slave, the negro was not merely severed from his own culture, he was psychologically shocked by the process, so that he was bound to become dependent upon his master, and his master's culture and social system in every possible way. Having lost the means of fending for himself in the world, he was forced into a Sambo stance, doing what his master bade him, being pathetically grateful for any kindness, and not even aspiring to any kind of independent life.

The first thing which we have to recognise about North American society therefore is that the fact of slavery was probably more important than the fact of the plantation system. And if, in fact, we think of a plantation as employing more than 20 slaves, only 12% of all slaveowners could be said to be running plantations, while 72% of slaveowners had less than ten slaves, and 50% had less than five.[12] What should perhaps be said is that there are certain features which are common to all men who are legally slaves, whatever sort of productive unit they work in, and that on the other hand there are differentiating features of the different kinds of system.

So far as the plantations were concerned, what is most striking is the extreme and amoral rationalism with which they were conducted. Far from it being the case, as Max Weber seems to imply, that only free labour is compatible with the rational calculating capitalist spirit, it would seem that the treatment of the slave as a thing or a resource, rather than as a man, was highly conducive to the development of a rational-calculating or utilitarian attitude towards him. Elkins indeed explains the emergence of the status of slavery in British and American law as following from the logic of unrestrained capitalism.

It is probably true, however, that slavery was never completely an economic institution in the sense that all of its features could be explained as being due to responses by the entrepreneur and employer to market opportunities. The owner of few slaves might, in fact, be engaged in what was an irrational form of enterprise or one which at best was able to give him a minimum income and status, and most discussion of the slavery question both amongst the whites and so far as we have any indication of this at all amongst the negroes, would be concerned not with the art on science of plantation management, but with the political, legal and moral aspects of slavery in general.

Much of what we can learn from Stamp,[13] who has given us the best-documented anti-slavery account of the North American institution, about the political and moral discussion

12. K. Stampp, *The Peculiar Institution*, Eyre and Spottiswoode, London, 1964, pp. 39–42.
13. *Ibid.*

of slavery by American whites can be matched in discussions by white settlers in Africa about the rights of the native African population. There is the same sense that the only argument that the underling ultimately understands is force, although the wise master is one who treats his men according to his own standards justly. There is the same belief that the servant or slave is better off as a servant or slave than he would be free and the sense that most know this and would be loyal were it not for the trouble-makers and agitators who stir the people up. And finally, there is the paternalistic belief that one's employee is a rather sub-normal child, who will steal and cheat because he doesn't really understand about morality, but who nonetheless has some of the charm of a child so that he should be treated with kindness and tolerance.[14]

These features are common to all situations where one group has absolute power over another, and it is important to our comparative sociological perspective to note that these simi-larities between slaveholding and non-slaveholding societies do exist. But it would be going too far to say that there was no difference. The difference lies in the legal definition of the slave's status. For beyond all the similarities between his subordinate status and that of the African worker in Southern Africa, there does remain the legal definition of the slave as a chattel and all that that implies, regarding his capacity to obtain manumission, his capacity to sell his labour, to own property, to enter into contracts or to have a legally binding marriage. In all these respects the position of the slave differs from that of other colonial workers, even though legal discrimination may exist and those rights which are accorded to the native worker may be derisory in the sense that he lacks the means to take ad-vantage of them. This formal legal freedom may profoundly affect the esteem in which a colonial people is held by others and even more the esteem which it accords to itself. The legal status of the slave, together with the violence which was used in

14. See, for instance, A. H. Richmond, *The Colour Problem*, Pelican, London 1955, pp. 150–54.

imposing that status on his ancestors, therefore, do make a difference and put the slave and even his remote descendants in a peculiarly lowly regarded position in any stratification system. This is a fact, more important than colour or racial characteristics, which may be obscured by the fact that all negroes tend to be regarded by whites in the former slaveholding countries as sharing in the stigma of slavery.

In discussing North American slavery even briefly as we have done, but much more in its extensive discussion by Stampp, it proves impossible to discuss the raw social relations involved in slavery (what Marxists would want to call the basis) without referring also to the belief systems, ideas, stereotypes and ideologies which are built into those structures. We should notice, moreover, that they make a difference to the actual nature of the institution itself. This becomes clear when we look at the comparison which is to be drawn between North and South American slavery.[15]

Tannenbaum has made the point that the difference between the two systems is a legal one, in that the Spaniards and the Portuguese approached the creation of their new multi-racial colonies in the Americas with a clearly defined legal conception of what a slave was. The North Americans, as Elkins points out, arrived at their conception of the slave through following through the logic of unopposed capitalism to its logical conclusions. The Spanish and Portuguese settlers found themselves with a pre-existing legal conception which defined the rights and the degree of rightlessness of the slave very clearly. More important even than the legal difference, however, was the moral pressure which could be brought to bear in consequence. The nature of the institution of slavery could not just be dictated by the courts to meet the interests of planters. It was a subject which had to be discussed by clerics and theologians whose opinions were held to matter by the government. As Nathan Glazer puts it in his introduction to Elkins' book:

In Brazil the church was powerful and insisted on the protection

15. F. Tannenbaum, *Slave and Citizen*, Vintage Books, New York, 1946.

of the slaves and the saving of souls . . . The royal government across the sea was also interested in the protection of the slaves. In any case the use of property in Latin American was hedged in by a variety of quasi-feudal restrictions and it was taken for granted that slaves were not the absolute property of their owners. In the Latin countries, in short, the remnants of feudalism protected the slave; in the society fashioned . . . in the United States nothing was left to prevent a cruelly logical reduction of the African to a piece of mere property.[16]

Glazer's point should not be misunderstood. It does not mean that the settlers and frontiersmen of Brazil or Latin America were morally any more pure than those who settled in North America and Africa and indeed they often expressed very similar sentiments. Thus one Spanish historian, contemporary with Las Casas, writes that the Indians are 'naturally lazy and vicious, melancholic, cowardly and in general a lying shiftless people. Their marriages are not a sacrament but a sacrilege. They are idolatrous, libidinous and commit sodomy. Their chief desire is to eat, drink, worship heathen idols and commit bestial obscenities'.[17] Nonetheless, despite this the institutions in terms of which the Spaniards and the Portuguese were able to organise their relations with the Indians and with the negroes were hedged around by restrictions which derived not from judgments made on the spur of a prejudiced and angry moment but from a mediaeval Catholic conception of man.

According to Tannenbaum the slave in Spanish society, 'had a body of law protective of him as a human being which was already there when the negro arrived and had been elaborated before he came upon the scene.'[18]

This code, Las Siete Partidas, allowed for the marriage of slaves, prevented the separate sale of man and wife, limited the powers which the master had to punish his slave and, perhaps above all made manumission very much easier than it was in

16. Elkins, op. cit., p. xii.
17. Gonzalo, Hernandez de Oviedo y Valdes quoted in L. Hanke, Bartolome de Las Casas, Martinus Nijhoff, The Hague, 1951.
18. Tannenbaum, op. cit.

North America. Indeed manumission became so normal and so frequent that Tannenbaum argues that

> In effect slavery under both law and custom had for all practical purposes become a contractual arrangement between the master and his bondsman. . . . Slavery had thus from a very early date at least in so far as the practice was concerned moved from a 'status' or a 'caste' by 'law of nature' or because of 'innate inferiority' or just because of the 'just judgment and provision of holy script' to become a mere matter of an available sum of money for redemption.[19]

This considerably overstates the case, and the inadequacy of Tannenbaum's categorisation of types of social structure can be seen from his designation of slavery as 'caste' and 'status' simultaneously. Nonetheless we can accept that the legal and ideological framework of the institution of slavery made a difference in the Latin countries. Not only is this important in relation to the kind of slavery which existed in Latin America. It also made a considerable difference to the race relations pattern which emerged in the aftermath of abolition. If it is true, as we suggested, that the negro's inferior position in the system of ethnic stratification was due to his association with a totally subjugated and unfree position as a worker, the lack of clear distinctions between slave and free which the Latin American system allowed would make equally difficult an absolute status distinction between white and coloured.

The presence of a large coloured population of mixed Indian, white and negro blood and the recognition of the coloured man as potentially the equal of the white made a further difference to Latin American society. In part this may be associated with Catholic teaching on marriage and a factor common to Spanish, Portuguese and French territories alike, but there is a special factor which affects the culture of the Iberian countries. This is that before they became great colonial powers both countries had been conquered by the Moors and had been subject to a considerable degree of miscegenation. There was no barrier in the way of the Portuguese and the Spanish settlers, not merely

19. *Ibid.*, p. 55.

having sexual intercourse, but actually marrying Indian and negro women, and the various American colonies had not been long in existence before the legitimate coloured offspring of Portuguese and coloured settlers took their place alongside those settlers at all social levels. By contrast in the United States such sexual relations as went on between white and black tended to be between white men and coloured women and the offspring would not be recognised as legitimate or as legally or socially sharing their father's status. The difference is striking enough to give support to Hoetink's thesis that the Spanish and Portuguese 'somatic norm image' included coloured people along with whites as being beautiful and socially acceptable.

The relative blurring of social and legal distinctions did not mean, of course, that there were no masters and slaves, no employers and employees, in Latin American society. There were plantations and smaller agricultural enterprises in Brazil as there were in the United States. But the Big House in Brazil as Freyre describes it was not simply a capitalistic economic enterprise cut off from other social institutions. It was a total society in itself.

The Big House completed by the slave shed represents an entire economic social and political system: a system of production (a latifundiary monoculture); a system of labour (slavery); a system of transport (the ox-cart, the bangue, the mock and the horse); a system of religion (a family Catholicism, with the Chaplain subordinated to the paterfamilias, with a cult of the dead etc.); a system of sexual and family life (polygamous patriarchalism); a system of bodily hygiene (the 'tiger', the banana stalk, the river bath, the tub bath, the sitting bath, the footbath); and a system of politics (*compradismo*).[20]

Even if one allows for Freyre's nationalistic pride in Brazil's rich and complex culture, it should be clear here that the exploitation of labour occurs here, as it doesn't in the case of the United States, within a complex normative and cultural framework. Although the orientation of activity in the Big House was

20. G. Freyre, *The Masters and The Slaves*, Knopf, New York, 1956, p. 7.

indeed towards production for the market, it still appears to have had other purposes besides. In fact this was an institution created by a dominant people whose culture was still full of feudal ideals and who could not produce a completely capitalistic social order.

We shall be returning later in this chapter to the specific rôle of the churches and their mission stations in relation to the system of economic production in Latin America and in the next chapter we shall consider what kind of an overall pattern these attitudes to slavery and the plantation produced. Before we do this, however, it is necessary to look at some of the other forms of employment of labour which colonialism has produced. We shall see that in some respects some of them are closer in spirit to North American antebellum slavery than the Latin American institution is. By the same token we shall argue that they are of more central concern to the student of race relations, or at least that the kind of race relations problem which they present has more in common with that of North America than that presented by Latin America even, though both North and Latin American social systems and culture are based on slavery.

The second major settlement by the English overseas took place at a difficult historical juncture. For, at the very time that these settlers were making their homes in Africa, the ending, not merely of the slave trade, but of slavery itself was being carried through. The interest of this period, therefore, lies in the alternatives adopted by the settlers in the creation of social institutions in the new colonial societies.

Alternative labour and agricultural systems were, of course, developed in North America after the defeat of the South in the Civil War, and these also had more in common with the North American slave system than that system had with its Latin American equivalent, at least as long as the migration of negroes to the North and to the cities was not possible. What experience in the Deep South after the Civil War seems to show is that the negro agricultural worker could be denied the possibility of free market activity so systematically that he was forced to do his master's bidding in order to live almost as completely as he had been under slavery.

The key to the subjection of the free plantation worker in agriculture is denial of access to the market either for the disposal of his product or for the purchase of his 'raw materials', seed, and tools, as well as his food supplies. These things, coupled with a deployment of political power by the ruling group to ensure that the ex-slaves did not exercise their new legal rights, were more than sufficient to keep the negro in a state of total subjection for many years after the abolition of slavery.

The plantation worker when emancipated was, of course, normally a wage labourer and had no direct access to the market. But a number of positions intermediate between those of labourer, tenant and free farmer were quickly developed, as the dominant white group stood between agriculturalists as such and their market. The central position is probably that of the share-cropper who sees the profit from a good part of his crop taken from him before it ever reaches the market. On the other hand, nearly all ex-slaves who became labourers, tenants or small-holders, found that they needed credit in order to get seed and equipment and that they would starve unless they were allowed credit in the plantation store. While in theory there was a way out of this through appeal to the courts, or through political action, the use of extra-legal violence and the substitution of lynch-law for the law of the state at the local level sufficed to ensure that the status of negro ex-slave in his relation with his white ex-master and the appropriate etiquette in master-servant relations were maintained.[21]

The situation of inferior groups in a formerly slaveholding society, however, is something of a special case. What we wish to suggest is that the post-slavery situation is not sufficient to explain modern patterns of subordination of inferior groups which are justified in racist terms, because similar types of subjection of peasants and workers have been arrived at in other colonial countries where there was never a set of institutions

21. G. Myrdal, *An American Dilemma*, Harper, New York, 1944.

parallel to those centring around slavery and the plantation, as there was in North America.

In the second period of European colonisation, the plantation played nothing like the central rôle which it had in the American colonies. The two primary forms of colonial exploitation were the purchase of crops from peasants and the establishment of mines. These created new patterns of superordination and subordination between colonising and colonised groups, some of which at least have gone to the shaping of 'race relations' patterns both in the colonial world and in the metropolitan countries.

The first inferior social position which might be imposed upon a colonial people arises in a somewhat negative way. We have already used the concept 'external proletariat' to describe the situation of a 'barbarian people' across the frontier. We now suggest that it may be used in a slightly more complex sense to refer to those people in a market-centred modernising society who remain outside the new pattern of activity and live wholly within the traditional subsistence sector.

As colonisers the British in particular were ambivalent about the extent to which they wished to see native peoples in colonial territories socialised into rôles appropriate to the new society. For one thing there were simply too many natives for the limited number of positions available. For another it was convenient to have a reservoir of workers to draw upon. For whichever reason, however, the institutions of indirect rule and of the reserve or reservation became normal features of British colonial society. That is to say that these societies became 'pluralistic' in a very special sense, namely that of having within them cultural enclaves where a 'primitive' and traditional culture and social system was permitted to co-exist with that of the new market-centred society.

Missionaries might seek with varying degrees of energy to enter these cultural enclaves and as we shall see later they helped to socialise and educate a steady stream of what are called in South Africa 'school-people' for entry into the society's main structures.[22] But, paradoxically, one result of this relatively incomplete missionisation of the reserved areas was simply to emphasise the difference between these areas and those which had become part of the imperial social system. Alternatively, it may be said that they served to reinforce the ambivalence with which the reserved areas were regarded, an ambivalence which finds its fullest expression in South African politics where one set of tendencies is directed towards forcing the native African out of his reserves to take employment in the towns, whereas another works for the enforcement of 'apartheid', which means, if it means anything, the maintenance of two economically and culturally unequal sectors in the same social system.

Between the subsistence peasant farmer in the reserved areas and the wage worker in the towns is the farmer who produces cash crops for the market. The important thing to notice about his situation is how remote his ultimate market is and how dependent he is on intermediaries. His exploitation does not have to depend upon any lynch-law. It is established by the fact of colonial conquest and the control of marketing facilities and the trade goods, which give meaning to the peasants' money, by the colonialist. The price for his crops is not fixed by haggling in the market, but simply by what the marketing organisation is willing to pay. Naturally these marketing organisations become one of the prime targets of revolutionary colonial nationalism and ready-made sources of plunder for the élites who take over when the colonialist is eventually expelled.

The next point to be noticed, as we make our way inwards towards the institutional centre of the market-oriented modernising society of the colonial towns, is a point which we might have made in relation to slaveholding societies. This is that one of the most common points of entry into the modern social system is not by employment in factories, offices or public works, but in domestic service. The position of the domestic servant, therefore, is one which requires our special attention.

The sociological key to the domestic servant's situation is that

22. P. Mayer, *Tribesmen or Townsmen*, Oxford, 1961.

a good part of his real income is provided in kind. This means that, instead of being able to engage directly in the rational calculation of market opportunities, which is of the essence of modern social order, he participates only indirectly through his master's *oikos* or household. It is the fluctuation of his master's income which determines his standard of living rather than what he can get on a free market for his labour. He will receive a token wage, but this wage has to be understood as akin to the pocket money which the master might give his child. The essence of the domestic servant's position indeed is that he is a child. And the essence of the master's position is that he is the paterfamilias of a household which includes more than simply kin.

There are a number of aspects of the domestic servant's situation in colonial contexts, moreover, which are suggestive of slavery. There is a tendency to tie him to his job through the introduction of penal sanctions against the servant who decamps. There is a considerable limitation on his own family life, since very often he is required to live in single quarters, and there is considerable similarity very often between the way in which a master talks of his servant or is permitted to punish his servant, and what occurs under the slave system. Most of what Stampp has to say about the ideologies and the extra-legal sanctions which supported the South's peculiar institution find their echoes amongst white Rhodesians discussing their servants in the nineteen sixties. Perhaps it is possible to argue that while the abolition of the slave trade and of plantation-centred slavery made a considerable difference to relations between agricultural and industrial workers and their employers, there was much more continuity between domestic slavery and domestic service as it emerged in colonial territories.

The most typical institution involving the use of native labour in Africa, however, is that of the mining compound. Curiously little has been written about this institution, perhaps because it still exists, and it is far more difficult to find support for detached academic investigation in the case of an institution which is still in full flower than it is in the case of a defunct institution like the slave plantation.

Compound labour is a form of contract labour and, in one respect, namely that of the shortness of its normal term, would appear to be freer than the contract labour, which took Indian plantation workers to grow sugar in British Guiana or South Africa. But in almost every other respect it is less free and more like the institution of slavery.

The starting point for entry into the compound labour system is a meeting with the recruiting company. This encounter, however, may be forced upon the colonial peasant because of measures which the government has introduced in order to force him out of the subsistence sector into mining and agriculture. The typical measures are those pioneered in Africa by Cecil Rhodes. The peasant is required under pain of imprisonment to pay a money tax, and the traditional landowning system which gave all members of the peasant community a right to subsistence is broken up, so that some at least are forced off the land. Apart from this, the post-conquest land settlement normally leads to a degree of overcrowding on the land which makes it increasingly impossible for the peasant to keep his family alive.

Under this kind of duress then, and lacking any means of checking whether the terms which the recruiting agent offers him can or will be honoured, he contracts to work for nine months. He is then taken to the city without his family, whom it is assumed will not need his moral or financial support because they are to be supported by the reserve economy, and he lives in a compound under lock and key in bachelor conditions. No union organiser or agitator can penetrate into his quarters, and, inevitably, his wages remain static even in times of inflation. These wages are not readily related to the cost of living, because the pattern of employment of this kind was laid down when the whole purpose of taking fixed employment was to earn money to pay a fixed tax rather than becoming a consumer in the urban market place.

Those who actually run the compounds would reject this ideal type of their sociological structure, and would argue that the worker is well cared for in the compound, and, indeed, that he has the advantage of having two sorts of income, one from his plot of land back home in the reserves, and the other from his employment. Two things may be said about this. One is that this kind of statement is very similar to paternalistic statements made by plantation owners when the Deep South system was at its harshest. The other is that the compound system in conjunction with the reserves system involves a kind of exploitation unknown to the plantations. For while the plantation owner had a perpetual responsibility for the upkeep of his slave, the mineowner, using compound labour, has no responsibility to his workers beyond the nine-month period.

Colonialism has rarely involved a substantial manufacturing sector based upon factory production and, hence, with our review of the plantation and slave system, of indirect rule and reservations, of marketing arrangements, of domestic servants and of compound labour in the extractive industries, we might be thought to have said all that there is to be said about the social structure within which production is carried on in colonial contexts. There are, however, a number of cases where industrial development has occurred on a considerable scale in colonial or post-colonial societies. Thus it is important that we say something of manufacturing industry as it operates in the conditions which prevail in the Deep South, in South Africa and in Latin America.

So far as the Latin American countries are concerned the problem of labour in the manufacturing industries is not primarily a race relations problem. There does, it is true, seem to be a tendency for negro labour to be concentrated in the lowest occupational strata, but this is not to say that a group is singled out on grounds of colour to suffer special disabilities which make it less free than any other group. Indeed the truth of the matter is that the political culture of the Latin American countries is less sympathetic to *any* workers having trade union bargaining rights, because it has a more feudal background than does the political culture of the English speaking world.

In North America again the pressure from federal sources, and the trend towards equality before the law for all workers, has prevented the development of substantial legal differentiation. This is not so, however, in South Africa, where a complex industrial system has arisen based upon legal differentiation of two kinds of labour.

The South African system[23] turns upon the basic fact of the Pass system, which requires that Africans should normally reside in the reserves, but may seek employment in the towns if they carry with them certification of the granting of permission to make a number of geographic and social moves. On this basis is built a whole system of restrictions on movement and limitation of the kinds of labour contract into which he can enter. In some industries he may be debarred by law from doing skilled work. In others he might be prevented from obtaining an apprenticeship. Finally, instead of having the right to trade union membership and collective bargaining, he is made subject instead to the paternalistic protective system offered by a Native Affairs Department. What all this means is that in the manufacturing industry there coexist a free white and an unfree black working class. There are, it is true, differences between the situation of the worker here described and the compound worker whom we have discussed above. Being able to live away from work and being able to have a family life are two important differentiating factors. Moreover these, taken together, mean the emergence of a native community and economy in which opportunities arise for small-scale business enterprise. Nonetheless the striking feature of the situation of the native worker in manufacturing in South Africa is the way in which his status is legally defined as unfree.

We cannot claim that this review of labour relations between workers and their employers, peasants and their customers is

23. van der Berghe, *South Africa, A Study in Conflict*, University of California Press, Berkeley, 1967.

comprehensive. It will nonetheless suffice to show that there are a whole range of employment situations in colonial territories in which workers and peasants of different physical or cultural characteristics from those who rule them are in a situation of unfreedom as compared with the workers of advanced industrial societies. It is not our thesis that this factor of unfree labour is the only structural factor underlying race relations problems. We do argue, however, that such institutional arrangements as we have been discussing are relevant to the understanding of race relations problems as well as the problem of plural societies. We cannot in fact accept either that the relations between the segments of a plural society or those between 'races' can be properly explained simply in terms of culturally differentiated social segments. We have shown here if we have shown nothing else, that there are not merely political but economic institutions which bind the various groups or segments together. They share their basic institutions. But with this said, we can readily go on to look at the structure of societies as they emerge objectively as well as in men's minds not merely at the point of production and employment but in society at large. For men do see themselves not merely as entrepreneurs, employers or workers working within productive establishments. They see themselves as members of ethnic groups having relations with other ethnic groups; they see themselves as members of urban society and community, and they see themselves as nations. It is to these larger units and the definition of statuses within them that we turn in our next chapter.

3. The Stratification and Structure of Composite Colonial Societies

The term 'stratification' is now so widely used in sociology without any kind of clarifying definition, that to question its use is to appear to be something of a sociological ignoramus. Yet there was a time when sociological theory used a far more precise language in talking about some of the structures which the term in its common usage appears to cover. It will be suggested here that it would be useful if we revised this more precise terminology, when we are seeking to delineate a society's overall structure, and, insofar as we wish to talk about composite colonial societies, that we should add to it. Before we do this, however, it will be useful by way of clearing the ground to list some of the main uses to which the term stratification is commonly put.

One use particularly common amongst reform-oriented sociologists in Britain and other European countries, seeking to establish a welfare state, is that which refers to the classification of the population in statistical categories by the sociologist. These categories referred primarily to income levels in the first instance, but attention switched later to inter-generation mobility, and to relationships such as that between parent occupation and income level attained. The categories were not thought of as groups or as collective actors of any sort, but were classifications made for his own purpose by the social statistician or sociologist. If the objection was raised that sociology was interested in social relations and groups rather than in the characteristics of discreet individuals, the approach would be given a semblance of theoretical respectability by a reference to Max Weber's notion that classes were to be distinguished by differential life-chances.[1] And it was indeed this concept with which social reformers were concerned and which provided a unifying link between a number of disparate studies.

Those who approached the study of society in this way, and with this very definite value perspective, commonly defended what they were doing by claiming that they were concerned with stratification as an 'objective fact' and not with mere subjectivity or 'false consciousness'. And the writer who was often thought of as most typical of the alternative and false subjectivist approach was W. Lloyd Warner. This was as a matter of fact, very unfair to Warner, who had specifically set out to show that there was a very high correlation between status ranking in terms of his Evaluated Participation and other subjective methods and the rankings which could be arrived at in terms of a weighted and composite index of status characteristics. But it certainly is true that Warner placed great emphasis upon the meaning of subjective status grading to the participants in a society, as did those American sociologists who proceeded to use occupational status gradings for a variety of purposes only after it had been shown that such gradings were subjectively accepted by the population at large.

What is perhaps more important about stratification studies in America, however, is not their subjectivity, but the fact that they were concerned with a particular subjectively held notion which might be expressed according to terminological preference by some term like 'status', 'esteem' or 'prestige'. The object of sociology appeared not to be the assessment of the relative life-chances of the individual, his powers in the market and so on. As in the case of the studies of differential life-chances, however, these studies did not necessarily carry the implication that the categories of individuals differentiated by the sociologist had any kind of corporate or communal existence.

In fact, the 'subjectivists' came to assert that what they were studying included all that was studied under the heading of life-

1. R. Bendix and S. M. Lipset, *Class, Status and Power*, Routledge and Kegan Paul, London 1967, pp. 21–8.

chances. Davis and Moore[2] for example, extended the term stratification to include not only studies of relative prestige, but of relative amounts of leisure and money, and, probably implicitly, political power as well. This is what they appear to be talking about when they say that the rewards necessary to recruit people to a social system and to motivate them to conformity include 'things that contribute to sustenance and comfort', 'things that contribute to humour and diversion' and 'things that contribute to self-respect and ego-expansion'.

What in fact has happened to stratification studies is they they have come to be concerned with the properties of systems. What Davis and Moore talk about is the reward system, and they go on to show that these rewards are accorded to individuals in accordance with the society's value system. The same notions are at the basis of Parsons' 'Revised Analytic Approach to Social Stratification'.[3]

It is not sufficient to dismiss such approaches as 'functionalist' or as based upon the notion of an unproven consensus, any more than it is sufficient to dismiss them as subjective. The point is, surely, that one possibility is that the members of a society carry around in their heads a conception of their society as a whole, in which rewards are allocated more or less justly in accordance with a system of values. It is important in any society that we should discover just what conception of the society as a whole individual social participants have. The really important criticism of the functionalist theory of stratification is that it contributes nothing to our knowledge of those societies, in which there is resentment of, and resistance to, the system of allocation of rewards, based upon a conception of the system as it is, and the system as it should be, and that secondly it says little about the complex structures whose perception leads to the formation of ideas of an overall stratification system. The latter point is of some importance and merits separate consideration.

2. *Ibid.*, pp. 47–53.
3. T. Parsons, *Essays in Sociological Theory*, pp. 386–439.

Max Weber[4] in what has remained one of the classic sources from which theorising about stratification starts, drew a distinction between class, status and party, and a more eclectic tradition of stratification theory than that of the functionalists now regularly makes the distinction between what are sometimes called the three dimensions of stratification. What relationship is there between these approaches and functionalist theory?

Max Weber perhaps confuses the issue somewhat by failing to distinguish between the operation of class, status and party, as elements in small-scale clearly delineated social structures, and the rôle of these factors in the formation of men's conception of society as a whole. This is a distinction which we would wish to make. Clearly, for example, it is true that wherever there is a market structure or something which can be usefully understood as a market structure, whether it be the market for capital, for housing, or for spouses, then one way of analysing that structure and its dynamics is to look at the way in which individuals are differentially placed with regard to their chances of obtaining control of the relevant resource. But it is also true that men think of society as a whole in terms of classes. That is to say that they have an image of society as a whole as some kind of market system, in which, because of their differential control of resources, men find themselves divided into groups with different and conflicting interests. Because they have these conceptions and images the group of those with like interests comes to act as what modern sociological jargon calls a reference group for its members.

Other images than that of the market may, however, be more important in particular societies at particular times in history. One is that which probably survives from feudal memory and which emphasises the division of society into groups with differing life-styles meriting varying degrees of honour or prestige. Another looks at the division of men according to the chance which they and their children have of gaining access not to positions of market power, but to decision-making positions in

4. Bendix and Lipset, *op. cit.*

the society. Both of these conceptions are very much in mind, for example, amongst British people when they discuss the question of social class and educational opportunity.

The more general notion of the class system of a society, to use the term which would be most widespread amongst laymen, or the stratification system, to use current sociological language, is based upon the assumption that, having taken all factors such as the organisation of society as a market, the organisation of society as a prestige system, and the organisation of society as a power system into account, the members, or a significant portion of the members, of that society then feel that it is possible to place themselves and other individuals in terms of some kind of a stratification system. This stratification system may be thought to involve distinct communal corporate groups or it may be thought of in 'conceptual' terms, that is to say that a concept of status position might be held without the implication that those who share a common position form any kind of group. In this latter case the scale of stratification positions is thought of as continuous.

If this analysis is correct, it would, of course, follow that what is important in their conception of the overall shape of society and its stratification system would differ for different social systems as well as for different groups of participants within a particular social system. Moreover, there may be some societies in which overall images of society are current which involve factors quite different from those relating to class, status and power which have so pre-occupied European and North American stratification theorists, and it might be that, at this point, what we have to do is to stop talking about stratification altogether, and simply say that the conception which members of a society have of society-as-a-whole is a significant factor which enters into the allocation of rights and rewards, and which affects the way in which one of the society's members acts towards another.

What we are suggesting really is this. Whereas Parsons or Davis speaks of the ultimate value system of a society as though this were a body of ideas not merely clearly and systematically articulated, but with clear particular applications at crucial institutional points in the social structure, we believe that in a great many contexts men operate with nothing more than an image of the immediate concrete social structure about them; but that they are also influenced, both in these immediate contexts and in thinking about, commenting upon and acting within overall social contexts, by a more or less clear but continually shifting picture of the total social order. It is only when they are confronted with the necessity of making forced verbal choices by sociologists that their ideas on this level take on a fixed and systematic character. Normally they are vague and unclear, differ between different groups, differ for the same man at different times and in different contexts, and have only a relatively poor articulation with particular and concrete institutional and group contexts. This is by no means to say that they are unimportant in explaining social processes. As we shall see shortly, they are very important in the understanding of colonial societies. But, precisely because they are so important, it is necessary that we should distinguish them from certain misleading implications of the notion of an ultimate value system.

Because sociology until very recently has been such an insular discipline, concerned with the problems of European and North American society, a great deal that has been written about men's images of society as a whole and about stratification has been about these societies, but, even here, there is a great deal of variation, both within the social images of a single nation, and between those of different nations. This can be seen by looking at the case of Britain and America.

In Britain several images of society as a system of 'classes' have conflicted with one another. One is that of class conflict between the 'working class' and 'the employers' which can be rationalised and systematised in Marxist terms, but usually spreads over from industrial contexts to provide a general picture of a society divided into 'them' and 'us'. This image, as

Elizabeth Bott puts it[5] this two-class power image, is widely current amongst manual workers and influences their responses when they are asked about 'class'. On the other hand socially mobile elements in Britain have always been frustrated by the closure of opportunities for mobility and entry into professional positions which carry high esteem and the opportunity to participate in significant decision making. To those whose view of society is determined by this experience, what matters is their exclusion by a closed group called 'the establishment' or 'the ruling class' and the crucial institutional area relevant to this discussion is the educational system. Finally, to many people, and particularly to housewives, what appears important is their own standing relative to that of other families as represented by life-style, especially in the form of housing, furnishings and possession of consumer durables. Any particular family which gets caught up in a debate about social class is likely to be influenced by all of these conceptions or by one or other of them according to context, and the socially mobile individual has an even more complex set of images to deal with, in that he still has reactions which derive from his earlier social context, at the same time as he is learning to play a new social and conceptual game.

By contrast with the British situation, the United States has no tradition of the labour movement being one of the major factors giving shape to the total social structure. Nor is it as much preoccupied with the closure of the social system at the top through institutions of educational privilege. In the absence of these factors as issues of public debate, the business of getting one's social orientations clear tends much more towards the pattern set by Riesman's 'other-directed man'. The status system becomes all important, and in the absence of highly prized residually feudal life-styles, what matters most in the estimation of a man is his style of consumption, i.e. what he can buy. On the other hand, there are elements in the American situation of which Britain has little experience. The most

5. E. Bott, *Family and Social Network*, Tavistock, London, 1958.

important of these are the absorption of immigrants and the existence of the colour-line. These two factors at least have to be taken into account as elements which would modify the American pattern and move it away from being a pure status system.

Neither the American pattern, nor the British one, however, is absolutely fixed and static, and neither of them is universally shared by all members of society, though, of course, quite commonly men might say, in effect, 'My own view is this, but I concede that the general view (or perhaps the ruling class view) is quite different. I will therefore take your questionnaire about the relative ranking of occupations to be asking not "What do you think?", but "what do you think that other people think?".' This is, therefore, a far cry indeed from any kind of functionalist approach which seeks to find out something about the ultimate value system of a society.

If what we have said is true, in the case of the relatively unitary advanced industrial societies, how much more is it likely to be the case in composite colonial societies? Quite clearly an East Indian in Guyana does not rank himself and his fellow Guyanese on any simple kind of stratification scale. He takes account of the fact that his parents were brought to the country as indentured labourers to work amongst ex-slaves and their children and their masters. He knows that his religion and culture are different from those of other people in the same society and that his physical appearance is different from that of some of his countrymen. Moreover, even within the group of Guyanese of East Indian origin, different individuals may adopt different views of the society as a whole, according to their educational standards, occupational rôle and degree of ac-culturation. It is of course, an empirical question of the first importance to ask what kinds of image of the total society vie with each other in the minds of the Guyanese. We simply wish to make the point that the historical situation is too complex for these social images to be predicted in advance from theoretical boxes whose headings and side-headings have been found to be exhaustive in the analysis of advanced industrial societies. Before we proceed to look more closely at the possibility of discovering some of the social images likely to be most useful in the understanding of composite colonial societies, there are three other issues which arise in our insular European and North American discussion of stratification, which we should consider, since such consideration is relevant to what follows. The first concerns the rôle of 'power' as an element in social stratification, particularly as that issue was posed in controversy about C. Wright Mills' work *The Power Elite*.[6] The second concerns the notion of power, facilities and rewards as being 'resources' of a system. The third concerns the extent to which any stratification or class theory implies the existence of actual historical groups of actors, rather than shadowy quasi-groups or reference groups.

Quite clearly even those who sympathise with the approach of C. Wright Mills to the study of the American system of stratification must recognise that he had difficulty in deciding what exactly he meant by power. It would seem that he wanted to arrive at an analysis which avoided the oversimplifications of Lloyd Warner's local analysis on the one hand and the crude categories of the Marxist theory of class conflict on the other. It seemed to him that the important thing was not that some Americans were in the social register, nor that they were a bourgeoisie locked in a class struggle with the organised working class, but that whereas a few men had power to take the big decisions (to produce or not produce, to make war or peace, to drop the bomb or refrain from doing so) the great mass of the population was an impotent and internally divided mass manipulated by the power élite and incapable of taking corporate action against them.

It would seem that in this model Mills sees the problem of power as one of who takes the important social decisions and particularly of who is capable of evading democratic control of his decision making. This is a relevant issue in a formally and theoretically democratic society. It is not particularly relevant

6. C. Wright Mills, Oxford, New York, 1959.

when we are dealing with a social order such as is to be found in the history of most colonial societies, where power means simply the power of life and death over another man, or the power to tell him what to do.

Interestingly Parsons criticises Mills' analysis of American society for precisely the opposite reasons to those which we are putting forward. He says

to Mills power is not a facility for the performance of function in, and on behalf of the society as a system, but is interpreted exclusively as a facility for getting what one group, the holders of power, wants by preventing another group, the 'outs' from getting what it wants. [7]

By contrast Parsons, being concerned as he is with the functional requirements of social systems, asks that power, like the two other categories of 'facilities' and 'rewards' should be treated as resources of the social system which are used in achieving the objectives of the system as a whole, as set out in its ultimate value system.

Mills, in fact, has a reply to this. There is a sense in which he is concerned with power as a resource of 'the system', but the system which he has in mind is that which the decision making directorate of society are seeking to bring into being for their own advantage. Thus, after appearing to deride the Parsonian system in *The Sociological Imagination*, he then goes on to say,

what Parsons and other grand theorists call 'value-orientation' and 'normative structure' has mainly to do with the master symbols of legitimation. This is, indeed, a useful and important subject. The relation of such symbols to the structure of institutions are amongst the most important problems of social science. Such symbols, however, do not form some autonomous realm within a society; their social relevance lies in their use to justify or oppose the arrangement of power and the positions within this arrangement of the powerful. [8]

Our comment on all this is that whether we regard power in

7. T. Parsons, *Structure and Process in Modern Societies*, Free Press, Glencoe, 1964, p. 220.
8. C. Wright Mills, *The Sociological Imagination*, Oxford, New York, 1959, p. 37.

terms of a 'zero-sum' game, as a resource used by a ruling class, or as a resource of the system, the important thing when we turn our attention to colonial society is the absence of overall value-consensus, the fact that one stratum or segment dominates the others, and that one of the dimensions on which the various segments or strata have to be differentiated concerns the degree to which they are legally free and capable of controlling their own economic destiny. In this sense we should say that power is an extremely important factor in colonial societies. If such distinctions are really viable, however, we should say that our concept of power is a zero-sum concept, since quite clearly the more one group has the less is available to the other.

The importance of these observations will become apparent as we move towards a typology of images of colonial social systems as wholes. The other question which we have to consider however, is that of the possibility that, as a result of men having certain social images, collectivities come into existence which can be thought of as social actors. We shall want to know whether the African population of South Africa or the East Indian population of Guyana can be thought of as being a real group and therefore having the capacity to take collective action, or on the contrary, whether the absence of structure, of formal organisation, of shared ideas and ideology, in a quasi-group of this kind, prevents it from acting in history, however much it may appear as a separate entity on the social map which people in the society concerned carry around in their heads.

Both Marx and Weber appear to have been aware of the importance of this problem. Weber repeatedly raised the question of whether or not groups differentiated in terms of market power or social honour could be thought of as real communal groups, and his conclusion seemed to be that the groups which actually acted in history were of a more specific kind.[9] Marx, on the other hand, looked in a number of literary, historical and political references at what he called, in Hegelian terms, the

9. M. Weber, *Economy and Society*, Vol. I, Chapter 4.

transformation of a class-in-itself into a class-for-itself.[10] By this he meant the process whereby those who shared the same situation in relation to ownership of the means of production came to be able to act historically. The Communist Manifesto can in fact be read as an account of how this process was carried through in the case of the European bourgeoisie and of how, at an accelerated rate, a 'similar process is going on before our very eyes' in the case of the proletariat.

The interesting point about this from our point of view, however, is that although classes are the prime historical actors in Marx's sociology he fails to establish clearly and convincingly what their structure is likely to be when they come to act. He speaks of the organisation of the workers first by their masters and then by their own trade union representatives. He suggests that the organised workers will unite their organisations at national and international level crossing local and industrial lines in doing so. And he suggests that the members of the class will come in varying degrees of clarity to share a consciousness of revolutionary objectives.[11]

In fact, in the case of classes in advanced industrial societies it has not happened this way, and the prime problem, indeed, which this aspect of Marxist theory raises, is the rôle of quasi-groups like social classes in our accounts of social structure. When we turn to the constituent elements of colonial society however, the constituent elements usually begin their career by having a distinctive structure and a distinctive culture. Thus, if it could be said that what was being produced was a class struggle, the various parties would be equipped from the start, through their ethnic organisations, with the means to engage in class struggle. On the other hand of course, the possibility of classes in the Marxian sense arising, which straddle and cross ethnic group boundaries, is even more limited.

10. K. Marx, *The Poverty of Philosophy*, Foreign Languages Publishing House, Moscow, p. 195.
11. K. Marx and F. Engels, 'The Communist Manifesto' in Marx and Engels, *Selected Works*, Vol. I, Foreign Languages Publishing House, Moscow, pp. 34–45.

We are now in a position to approach the question of the stratification and structure of composite colonial societies. What we shall be concerned with is the way in which people within these societies see them to be differentiated and composed, and whether the images of this differentiation and composition lead to action by the various groups which these social images posit as existing. The whole point of our discussion of European and North American stratification theory has been that, in the case of those societies, it was in the area of class and stratification that the major images of social systems as wholes were formulated. Whether or not stratification is the best or most useful word to apply to the forms of differentiation and composition in colonial societies is something which we shall have to decide in the light of the discussion which follows.

In the previous chapter we began by discussing the institutions of production in colonial societies and drew attention to the fact that such institutions are brought into being after some kind of military conquest or other use of force and that they rest upon some form or other of unfree labour. Men in such societies have very clear images of the concrete institutions involved. They are enshrined in legal codes. Their nature is continually discussed and defined by the punishment of those who deviate from the norms. What we now have to do, however, is to show how over and beyond these images an image of the wider society emerges. This will involve looking at the various other parties who emerge in colonial contexts, and at the way in which social images are extended to include these other parties, as well as to bring together in one group men who are not bound together within the same productive establishment. We do not take the view that such wider social images derive simply and directly from the social relations of production. Other factors certainly affect their formation. We do insist, however, that the social relations of production are one important factor and we shall at least, by virtue of the fact that we have singled them out for separate treatment, avoid oversimplifications like that which suggests that the various ethnic segments of colonial society have totally separate sets of institutions, apart from the political sphere.

The colonial encounter, which we have hitherto assumed, has been based upon the simple notion of two parties. These have been thought of as the colonialists, on the one hand, and natives or imported labourers, on the other. We now have to see that nearly every other colonial society includes a number of other component elements, partly arising from the social division of labour, but partly having come into existence and then being assigned a position in the division of labour. Amongst the issues we shall now have to discuss are the distinction between colonial officials and settlers, the rôle of secondary colonialist and traders, the emergence of mixed populations as a result of inter-breeding between masters and servants and the rôle of religious missions.

It is by no means to be assumed that the establishment of a colony by the European powers in Africa, Asia or America has meant merely the composition of a new society out of a unitary colonising element on the one hand and some sort of native or imported labouring population on the other. Quite obviously the business of managing the new society politically and economically involves a considerable division of labour, and, though the extent of this division of labour may vary con-siderably from one colonial situation to another, in all but the simplest cases it opens up the possibility of divisions of interest arising amongst the colonisers. Obviously it is in the very nature of capitalist societies that entrepreneurs in the economic sphere are not necessarily responsive to the wishes of government officials so that one would in any case expect some conflict between the political and economic authorities. Much more important than this kind of conflict, however, is that which arises when settlers from the metropolitan country go out to the colony as workers or as farmers. Such settlers are in direct conflict with the native population and any imported population based on contract labour while at the same time bringing with them the kinds of conflict with business and the government which had existed in a metropolitan context. Where there is such a settler element therefore a special dimension is added to colonial problems.

The country par excellence in which the new composite society is dominated by a settler element is South Africa. With one in five of its population being of European origin it surpasses all others in the sheer relative size of its settler population. And this settler population, having won its freedom from any kind of dependence upon colonial officialdom or interference from the metropolitan country, has succeeded in making itself the ruling segment in a plural society. As against various half-hearted and unsuccessful attempts by the British government to establish what were called multi-racial societies, the policy of white supremacy seemed entirely successful in the late sixties, though this is not to say that internal forces, aided by armed forces from across the country's borders, could not change the balance of power and overthrow white supremacy.

The interesting thing about the settler government of South Africa, however, is its class basis. Capitalist interests in the country could, subject to certain guarantees about the continued availability of cheap unskilled labour, fairly readily accommodate themselves to African rule and to the expulsion of those settlers whose presence was not strictly necessary from an economic point of view. But the white working class, fearing competition of cheap black labour, and farmers, unable to compete with industry in what it is prepared to pay its African workers, have succeeded in organising themselves in defence of their economic interests as they see them. Thus the so-called Nationalist Party in South Africa is as much as any party in the world a class-based party, and one which has become sufficiently strong in the grip which it has on the settler electorate to force local and absentee white capitalists to respect the rule of white supremacy.

In such circumstances there can, of course, be no unified working class movement in the Marxist sense. What the white worker and farmer government has set about doing is to restrict the entry of African labour to the towns and to ensure by one means or another that it is restricted to unskilled and semi-skilled work. Because of the restricted conditions under which such workers work and live, moreover, there is little chance of their becoming effectively organised in a trade union or party sense. Potentially they, like the white workers, are classes-for-themselves as much as the white working class actually is, the two classes being distinguished by the fact that they have differing degrees of control of the means of production. But the system of political controls ensures that they will remain disorganised.

What we are saying here is that in those cases where there is a large settler population including farmers and employed workers living in a colonial context, then the farmer and settler element amongst the settlers is likely to form a class in something like the Marxian or Weberian sense and defend its interests not merely in the market but in the political sphere. Native labour is thus forced into a position of having less control over the means of production and is potentially a separate class. Its capacity to act in defence of its interests however, is severely restricted by the political regime which the white politically organised class is able to establish.

There are, it is true, other dimensions to settler governed societies, but it must surely be recognised that they are marked by a particular form of class struggle, that is to say a conflict between physically distinguishable groups acting in terms of their material interests. It is not simply a difference in the set of institutions possessed by these two. Nor is it correct to describe them simply as castes. Whatever else is the case, it is clear that one of the features of these two groups is that they are classes in a capitalist society.

The South African situation is not repeated in the same degree anywhere else in the world. Only Algeria had a settler population approaching that in South Africa in its size relative to the native population. In the Algerian case the native population were able to defeat the colon element in a revolutionary war, and thereupon revealed the divisions which exist between the native working-class, the peasants and other elements in a nationalist movement. In other cases there was a struggle for ascendancy between a relatively small settler population and a colonial officialdom which had no interest in protecting pure settler interests, however much it might seek the alliance of a native bourgeoisie or other class which might be counted on to give guarantees to businesses, which wished to continue to operate in a post-colonial or neo-colonial context.

Apart from settlers from the metropolitan society the colonial conquest opens the way for other secondary colonialists. These include capitalist entrepreneurs seeking opportunities in mining, in manufacture and marketing, small-scale traders and shopkeepers and workers having a greater degree of freedom than the native workers or slaves who preceded them. In some cases these elements may come to constitute a half or more of the population and the achievement of independence from colonial rule still leaves unresolved the conflict between the basic worker and peasant population and the secondary colonialists. Indeed it might be said that only under the rule of the original metropolitan power was it possible for these elements to live together in a single society. This is clear both from the strains which have arisen after independence in such countries as Guyana, Mauritius, Singapore, Malaysia and Indonesia, where any bid to take political power by the secondary colonialists might very well lead to their violent extermination.

The social structure which is maintained in societies of this kind under colonial rule is sociologically speaking a little difficult to classify. The fact that the groups of differing national or ethnic origin which constitute the population are also in some degree occupationally specialised is suggestive of a caste or estate system of some kind. Yet it is as clear that there is no common ideology or value system in such a society, as it is that all groups participate in, and are united by the same economy. It would perhaps be best to refer to a society of this kind by some special term like colonial estate system or ethnically plural estate system. Again the use of such a term might serve to draw attention to the fact that more is at stake than merely the cultural and institutional differences between the component groups in the population.

One particular element which occurs in these societies, as it does in metropolitan societies, is the existence of groups who perform rôles which are held in some way to be morally dubious. This is particularly true of groups which engage in small-scale trading operations. The Indian traders of East Africa and the Syrians and Lebanese in West Africa provide good examples. They may be said to constitute a pariah element in the societies of which they form a part and in times of trouble and difficulty they might well serve as a scapegoat both to the ruling colonialist element and to the local working population.

Societies of this sort appear to be precariously placed in the event of the withdrawal of the major colonising power. At this point it becomes apparent that the protection under which the various groups lived, and the order which existed between the groups, depended upon a monopoly of the means of legitimate violence in the hands of the colonising power. Moreover, insofar as there was any evaluated social ranking of the groups, this was not something which arose because of an overall consensus. Rather it depended upon what was important and 'functional' for the colonising power.[12] In the post independence situation, unless a de facto agreement can be reached to the effect that while one party should have a monopoly of governmental power, the other may be permitted to dominate the economic sphere, the likelihood is that the various ethnic segments, estates or strata which have been brought together artifically by the colonial power will vie for political domination. There have been de facto agreements to divide power in some of the most crucial cases, as in Malaysia, but, after only a decade or so of independence, it appeared that these agreements were breaking down.

So far we have assumed that colonialists and settlers on the

12. On the question of 'Functional for whom?', see Furnivall, *Colonial Policy and Practice*, *op. cit.*

one hand, and natives and immigrant workers on the other, do not intermarry and that their cultures remain distinct. A striking feature of nearly all colonial societies, whether the colonisers approve intermarriage or not, is the emergence of a population with a mixed biological inheritance, but speaking the language and with variations practising the culture of the dominant group. Examples of such populations are the *mulatto* population of Brazil, the *mestizos* of Mexico and the Cape coloureds of South Africa. In some cases such populations have been the result of exploitative sex relations between colonialists and natives or slaves and the offspring are not acknowledged as belonging to the colonialists' group. Alternatively it might be the policy of the colonialists to intermarry and a merging of physical types might occur with some people with mixed race characteristics being recognized as belonging to the ruling group and entitled to acceptance in the highest social circles.

The merging of cultures and the merging of physical types does create important new sociological possibilities. Instead of a society in which a number of ethnically distinct groups are arranged in some sort of overall hierarchy in terms of the degree of protection which they enjoy from the dominant power, with status gradations occurring only within each group and in terms of its own internal criteria, we have here a breaking down of the boundaries, and the possibility, through the emergence of a shared culture, of a stratification system which incorporates two completely distinct groups at its two extremes, and which allows for an infinite number of gradations in between.

This is to say that the colonial estate system is not the only possible destiny for a composite colonial society. Intermarriage, coupled with the adoption of the colonisers' culture by the half-breed population, might well permit the emergence of a system of status grading more akin to that of a unitary society. In the North American case and in the South African case, of course, it is denied that there is any continuity either physically or culturally between coloured and white groups, and the coloured group is assigned to its particular level in the colonial estate system. But colour differences may be taken account of in a quite different way, in that a continuous colour gradation may be seen as the index of a continuous status gradation. Thus we see that composite colonial societies might be structured in terms of class conflict, in terms of a particular kind of estate order, or in terms of continuous status gradations. Moreover, any particular society may involve all three principles in some degree. But crosscutting these essentially stratification principles is another, namely that of the degree of acculturation to a particular cultural pattern.[13]

It is true, of course, that there are some societies in which such an acculturation process does not occur to any marked degree. But it is also the case that at least in the case of those colonising powers which have professed Christianity, missionaries have accompanied the colonisers and have sought, not merely to convert the heathen, but also to teach them the metropolitan culture. This was the purpose of the *aldeiamentos* of Brazil as it was of the mission stations in South, Central, and East Africa.

Exactly what the rôle of the missions has been on balance will no doubt be a matter for dispute between historians. Some still emphasise the fact that the missions acted as a curb on the settlers and protected native people from the cruder forms of exploitation. Some would emphasise that the missions acted as acculturising agents helping to create a social order that rested on something more than force. Some would maintain that the effect, if not the deliberate intention, of these acculturising activities was to make the natives more completely available to settler exploitation.

It is undoubtedly true that whatever else the effect of mission education was, it imposed upon its pupils a belief in the virtue of precisely that kind of disciplined work which was necessary if

13. It is surprising that van der Berghe, who is well aware of these various dimensions, as is shown by his *South Africa, a Study in Conflict*, should employ the somewhat simplistic distinction between paternalistic and competitive systems in his *Race and Racism*, Wiley, New York, 1967.

they were to be recruited as workers to settler-run industry and agriculture. This was likely to happen even though the missionaries saw themselves as protecting their charges from this kind of exploitation. In Brazil the Jesuits achieved a curious compromise. What they did was to take young Amerindian boys and successfully deculturise them in the sense of cutting them off from their own people without necessarily giving them a footing in the main Portuguese culture or the Brazilian culture which was coming into being. As Freyre describes the process:

> The untutored Indian lad was taken out of savage life by the padre when he had no more than his milk teeth with which to bite the hand of this bringer of civilisation, when he had as yet no definite code of morality and his tendencies were vague in character. He, it might be said, was the axis of missionary activity; it was out of this lad that the Jesuit was to fashion the artificial being so dear to his heart. ... The culumium or Indian lad became the accomplice of the invader in drawing the bones, one after another, from the native culture, in order that the soft portion might be the more readily assimilated to the patterns of Catholic morality and European life ...[14]

This was a more humane process no doubt than the middle passage but in its cultural effects it was no less devastating. But as Wagley and Harris point out the acculturation process was not finally carried through.

> In these Jesuit *aldeiamentos* the missionaries did not attempt to impose a change from an aboriginal tribal culture to the western culture of the time. Rather did they attempt to impose what might be called a 'Jesuit culture' distinct from the culture which had taken form in the rest of the colony.[15]

The cultural half-way house was symbolised by the fact that the Jesuits taught them to speak not Portuguese but Tupi, the Indian language which they had made into the *lingua franca* of the Indian tribes. Yet Wagley and Harris emphasise that the

14. Freyre, *op. cit.*, p. 142.
15. Wagley and Harris, *op. cit.*, p. 28.

missionaries taught the Indians 'new occupations and new work habits' and as Boxer tells us they were reluctantly compelled to allow the inmates of the *aldeias* to perform manual labour for the Portuguese colonists, under certain conditions and safeguards.[16]

The process was completed when the Jesuits were expelled and the Indians, no longer able to return to a full-blooded tribal culture and social system, either tried and often failed to cope with life on reservations, or gave themselves up to the settlers as a new labouring population.

Oliver suggests an even more direct process of disciplining the liberated slaves who were assembled by the missionaries in the mission stations of East Africa:

In their schools, life was regulated almost as severely by the mission bell as it was in England by the factory hooter. It summoned the children to prayer at sunrise, to work at 6.30, to religious instruction and rest at 11.00, to work again from 2.30 till sundown. Having assembled once more at the foot of the altar to thank God for his mercy, they were left to themselves till 9.30, when 'at a signal from the Father, conversation ceased and all sought rest in sleep'.[17]

Clearly then, whatever the stratification dimension along which the various native peoples and imported slaves and labourers were to be arranged, they could also be looked at in accordance with their degree of acculturation, although as Mayer has so interestingly pointed out in his study of East London in South Africa[18] in the aftermath of missionisation, urbanisation and industrialisation, the African population remained divided into two clear groups which he calls 'Reds' and 'School-people'. The Reds aggressively asserted their tribal culture, wearing European clothes for work but red blankets for best. The school-people remained locked in the missionary culture which they had

16. C. R. Boxer, *Race Relations in the Portuguese Colonial Empire 1415–1825*, Oxford, Clarendon Press, 1963, pp. 89–90.

17. Roland Oliver, *The Missionary Factor in East Africa*, Longmans, London, 1967, p. 52.

18. P. Mayer, *op. cit.*

achieved, practising the Puritan virtues and wearing the styles of clothing which the missionaries had deemed respectable at the turn of the century.

It will be remembered that the question which we posed for ourselves earlier in this chapter was that of the conception or conceptions of the total social system which were current amongst men and women at different points and levels of colonial society. We wanted to know what the equivalents were of 'the three class status model' or 'two class power model' in terms of which colonial people thought about their society as a whole. We recognised that the relevant models might include dimensions which could not adequately be summed up under some term like stratification.

The first thing to note in answering this question is that even less than in the advanced industrial countries colonial people did not have one shared view on these matters. How they looked on the world differed according to whether or not they had entered the Western money economy, whether or not they had accepted the religion of the colonising power, whether they were rich or poor, old or young, and a host of other factors of this kind. In the long run, of course, the establishment of a new society would depend upon a limited number of sociological world views being widely shared, but it is by no means certain that every composite colonial society will eventually survive. What one might be witnessing in the immediately post-colonial period is the break-up of a number of sociologically non-viable units.

It has to be noted furthermore that the problem of understanding the main subjectively defined dimensions of colonial societies is a twofold one. In the first place there is the problem of defining the kind of order which exists so long as the reins of political power are still in the hands of the prime coloniser. But separately from this there is the problem of predicting what is likely to happen after his departure. No doubt, for example, there is a specific sociological picture which can be drawn of India under the British Raj. As Annan has pointed out, Rudyard

Kipling was its sociologist as well as its poet.[19] But the structure of Indian culture after independence is quite another matter even though one element which would enter into it would be the imitative British quality of some of its institutions.

The first thing to be said about the colonial order during the stage when the prime colonisers were present, is that there was a sense of imposed order. On the one hand there was no perspective of resisting the colonisers by force except through the intervention of some divine and native agency. Cargo cults there might be from time to time, but in the long run when prophecy failed, it would be clear that there was in fact little chance of throwing the white man into the sea. Whatever else then, the new society would be one which was to his liking.

This new order would appear to the native or to the labourer, the peasant or the slave in terms of a division of labour between the various agents of the colonising process, especially the soldier, the official, the settler and the missionary. If he had not suffered too severe a physical or cultural 'middle passage' the individual in the colonies might succeed in retaining his own domestic and communal culture even while participating as worker in the new economy. But quite commonly in some degree he would be drawn towards and influenced by the culture of the colonisers.

The cultural pluralism of colonial society may in fact be looked on in two ways. It is an oversimplistic view which represents the social order in the colonies as resting simply upon a number of culture patterns of differing historical origin. This dimension is of course there, but there is also a striking difference between men according to the degree in which they are trying to assimilate and be accepted into the social order of the colonisers.

This social order, of course, is not simply a cultural system based upon religious practices, forms of family life and morality, ways of cooking and eating. There is this dimension, but these

19. N. Annan, *Kipling's Place in the History of Ideas*, collected in *Victorian Studies*, Vol. III, 1959–60 by Andrew Rutherford, published by Oliver and Boyd.

are aspects of the coloniser's social order which are least readily absorbed. What is far more important is the way in which he invites those whom he governs to share his view of the relative degrees of power and esteem which are to be accorded to the different segments of the society.

There is, of course, no shared and unitary view of this stratification system. The present author suggested in an earlier work that in any social system the main institutional pattern was likely to be a compound product consisting of ruling class proposals and the reactions of the ruled.[20] Moreover, he raised the question about status systems of who it was who was accorded the esteem and by whom. There is even more reason for making these distinctions in colonial society, for here one has the ruling groups proposals as to how the world should be viewed, the acceptance or rejection of these proposals by various groups, the elaboration of counter-conceptions and the cynical play-acting acceptance of the ruling class order in order the better to manipulate the ruling group to one's own advantage.

What the ruling group proposes is that the various segments should be seen as forming some sort of hierarchy according to their cultural and historical past. This would include, on the one hand, some evaluation of the group's own historical culture and its adaptiveness to work and to the coloniser's culture, and, on the other hand, an evaluation of the various groups according to the degree to which they have been able to resist subjection. Evaluations of this kind were particularly important in the debates which went on between priests and politicians in Latin America about the rightful position of Indians as compared with negroes. They are still important in South Africa where Nationalist politicians of Calvinist persuasion still debate the different destinies to which God is thought to have called African, Indian, Coloured, English-speaking and Afrikaans-speaking people.

Needless to say, this order is not immediately and readily

20. J. Rex, *Key Problems of Sociological Theory*, Routledge and Kegan Paul, London 1961, pp. 122–31.

accepted by the whole population. No group will whole-heartedly accept its own assignment to the lowest rungs on the social ladder. But survival in day to day transactions with the colonisers may well lead some to give the appearance of accepting this view of society, while there will be others for whom what might be called the Sambofication process has gone so far that their own self-image is that which is derived from taking the 'white man's' view.

The coloniser's culture pattern affects the new society not merely in terms of the status order which it proposes as between the various segments. It also proposes a new scale of values in terms of which each segment may evaluate and grade its own members. Since these segments already have their own internal value system in terms of which gradings are made, the situation becomes immensely complex. Thus, for example, it might be that within the particular segment there is some ambiguity as to whether a man of superior lineage is to be treated as the superior or inferior of a headmaster of 'humble origins'. Compromises are worked out in matters like this, and these compromises serve to create the day to day status evaluation system within the particular segment. There is, however, an ambivalence about such a system and it is to be expected that individuals will from time to time resolve it by compulsive emphasis upon either tradition or modernising patterns.

But it is not merely a status order which the colonising power proposes as between the segments and within the segments. At least as important is the economic order. This may involve the development of class conflict, according to the relationship which different groups have to the means of production, or it may involve the establishment of what we have called a colonial estate system based upon relative acceptance of occupational specialisation by the various segments.

Class conflict, when it occurs, takes many and complex forms. In particular, ethnic differences between native and settler or between the various kinds of colonial worker prevent the emergence of overall working class solidarity. It is quite natural then that, having failed to win support from his fellow worker, the colonial worker might look to his own ethnic group for defence. True, not everyone within that group and its organisations shares his economic status, but those who don't are likely to feel deprived by the colonial system in other ways, and are more willing to fight the worker's battles for him than are his fellow workers from another group. Thus class-struggle becomes merged in the nationalist struggle, but the nationalist struggle is itself transformed by this merging process. There may in the long run be battles to be fought between the colonial workers and the colonial bourgeoisie, but these are in any case less acute than European Marxists represent them to be and than the present conflicts which they have with fellow workers from other ethnic groups, and can readily be left to be resolved in the future.

Finally, one may arrive at relative stability under the colonial regime, if each of the various groups including not only workers but settlers and secondary colonialists achieve a kind of caste-like accommodation to one another. This has never happened completely but it has always happened in some degree. And it has happened most particularly in those countries where the residue of feudal ideology has prevented the development of full blooded capitalism and full blooded class warfare.

Thus what we have in the case of composite colonial societies is a social order which, as it is subjectively understood by those who participate in it, is less stable, more violent, more un-predictable and less easily summed up under the traditional categories of stratification theory than is any advanced in-dustrial society in a metropolitan country. But we must now ask one final question in this chapter: What is the relationship be-between these divisions and conflicts, as well as the forms of integration to be seen in colonial society, and the problems of race relations?

We shall, in fact, argue in later chapters that situations such as these need not in fact be seen in racial terms at all, and, par-ticularly in those cases where intermarriage and cultural merging are coupled with feudal conceptions, this is less likely. But it is

the case that in the concrete social institutions which we discussed in the second chapter, as well as in the conceptions of the
whole social order which we have discussed in this, there is
sufficient ambiguity and conflict, sufficient resentment and injustice for the system to require some further ordering and
rationalisation. This is achieved through the unequal treatment
of various racial groups, which may be called racialism and by
the adoption of deterministic belief systems about the differences between the various ethnic groups, segments or strata,
that is to say, racism. We shall look at the problems of racialism
and racism in our final chapters. But, before we do this, we shall
have to consider the structural bases of these phenomena not
only in composite colonial society but in the metropolitan
industrial societies themselves.

4. Minorities in Metropolitan Society

So far we have been considering colonial societies and their social structures only. We have drawn attention to the composite nature of these societies, arguing that they emerge almost universally as the result of conquest, and that they contain segments based upon the ethnic units brought together by the original conquest, even if these segments are nothing more than polar points between which there is a continuous grading of physical and cultural difference. We have also emphasised that such systems rest to a large degree on coercive sanctions deployed by the ruling group in its dealings with those whom it rules. In all these respects colonial societies differ from the advanced metropolitan industrial societies, from which the colonial conquerors came. In sum, we may say that what distinguishes the colonial social order from the metropolitan one is the clear ethnic pluralism, and the very much greater reliance on coercive sanctions in the former than the latter.

The fact of pluralism and the fact of these coercive sanctions make it more likely that the unequal treatment meted out to members of different groups in the colonial case will come to be characterised by racist ideas and beliefs and by racialist practice. We shall see in later chapters how most colonial societies develop in this direction. What we now have to do, however, is to consider whether, despite the greater tendency in metropolitan societies towards cultural unity, value consensus and the use of normative sanctions, there are nonetheless possibilities within even these societies of the development of those structural and ideological features which might be identified as conducive to the development of a race relations problem.

From what has already been said in earlier chapters, it will be clear that we see the pattern of stratification in industrially advanced metropolitan countries as very complex indeed, far too complex for it to be thought of in simple unidimensional terms. To mention only the most obvious aspects, there is the class dimension involving both a differentiation of life-chances and the formation of groups amongst those similarly placed for the defence of their interests; there is the status dimension in terms of which those who have certain valued characteristics are accorded greater esteem than those who lack them or have them in lesser degree; and finally there is the power dimension in terms of which some individuals are capable of commanding the behaviour of others.

The question now is whether, despite this complexity, there is some sort of trend towards 'integration' in the basic structure of the advanced industrial countries and, if so, what the nature of that trend is. We believe that there is such a trend, and that the peculiar position of minorities in these countries arises from the fact that they are unintegrated minorities in a relatively stable and integrated social order. But precisely because we do believe this, it is important to avoid oversimplification as to the nature of the integrative mechanisms.

Much of the literature on social stratification is in fact misleading because it appears to suggest that the second of the two factors mentioned above, that of status gradations, is the all important one. This is not a charge which can be laid at the door of Davis and Moore or Talcott Parsons in that they specifically see the unequal differentiation of prestige as only one aspect of the society's reward system, but their work has too often been read as referring solely to the status dimension.

A basic difficulty with the functionalist theory as it was first developed by Davis and Moore, however, is that it seems to do insufficient justice to the elements of conflict, bargaining and contract to be found in the society, and that, however useful it might be in explaining the functioning of some ideal social order, it cannot by itself explain the actual behaviour of people in, say,

British or American society. The question is, therefore, whether a more comprehensive and inclusive theory could be arrived at by starting from another point, and this would appear to mean starting from economic differentiation and from market power and political power.

Parsons is very well aware of the extent to which actual stratification systems differ from that to which his ideal type refers. Moreover he is clear that the factor of power must be introduced to explain these discrepancies. As he puts it,

It is convenient to conceptualise this element of discrepancy between the normatively defined 'ideal' ranking order and the actual state of affairs in terms of the ranking in value terms and 'power'. Power we may define as the realistic capacity of a system-unit to actualise its 'interests' (attain goals, prevent undesired interference, command respect, control possessions, etc.) within the context of system interaction and in this sense to exert influence on processes within the system.[1]

The consequence of this maldistribution of power is the development of a state of affairs in which some of the actors in a social system are insufficiently motivated to succeed in terms of seeking the kinds of rewards which the society offers:

In the lower reaches of the structure there are tendencies to deviation from the middle-class pattern. ... Essentially we might say that this consists in a shift from the predominance of the success goal to the security goal. More concretely it is a loss of interest in achievement, whether for its own sake and for the opportunity to do more important things, for the advancement of family status through more income or increased reputation. Occupational rôle then becomes not the main field for achievement, but a means of securing the necessities of a tolerable standard of living, a necessary evil.[2]

With this formulation Parsons seems to recognise an element of class struggle in advanced societies, albeit of a defensive kind. The point, however, is whether this can or should be introduced simply as a deviation from a smoothly functioning ideal type. Is

1. Parsons, *Essays in Sociological Theory*, p. 390.
2. *Ibid.*, p. 434.

it not the basic fact about advanced industrial societies against the background of which the emergence of a relative value consensus becomes understandable? This much seems to have been understood by Lipset in his *Political Man*[3] and by Daniel Bell in the *End of Ideology*.[4] At least Lipset sees the essential step towards emergence of this consensus as being the political incorporation of the working class,

> The characteristic pattern of stable Western democracies in the mid-twentieth century is that they are in a post-politics phase – that is, there is relatively little difference between the democratic left and right, the socialists and the moderates, and the conservatives accept the welfare state. In large measure the situation reflects the fact that in these countries the workers have won their fight for full citizenship.
>
> Representatives of the lower strata are now part of the government groups, members of the club. The basic political issue of the industrial revolution, the incorporation of the workers into the legitimate body politic, has been settled. The key domestic issue today is collective bargaining over differences in the division of the total product within the framework of a Keynsian welfare state and such issues do not require or precipitate extremism on either side.[5]

But Lipset's view of the nature and operation of the value system of the post-political phase of industrial societies is somewhat naïve. There is no explanation as to why the step from conflicting to agreed political aims should have been taken and there is no consideration of the relationship between the agreed goals to which he refers and other aspects of the society's value system. These issues are especially important to us since we will be considering the way in which groups of immigrants confront the consensus from outside and the prospects which they in their turn will have of 'incorporation'.

It is obvious at once that there is a considerable difference between the kind of values which form the basis of Lipset's consensus and those which form the basis of Parsons'. The former

3. S. M. Lipset, *Political Man*, Heinemann, London, 1960.
4. D. Bell, *The End of Ideology*, Free Press, Glencoe, 1960.
5. Lipset, *op. cit.*, pp. 92–93.

include on the one hand the material goals of occupational classes, and on the other the positive value which the parties attach to the system that enables them to realise these goals. In other words the emphasis is on instrumental values. Parsons on the other hand is concerned with the criteria in terms of which the units of a social system are ranked and these criteria cannot be reduced to purely instrumental values.

In fact both types of value are important in the creation of consensus in capitalist or post-capitalist societies, and it is important to discover the relationship between them. We think that this is best done by referring to the conflict system out of which the value system of what Lipset calls the post-political period has arisen. When we do this we see that the value system of the advanced capitalist societies is a complex structure of ideas and norms including ruling class values in terms of which a ruling class seeks to impose its own ideal social system on the population at large; a set of countervalues which arises in what Parsons calls 'the lower reaches of the structure', as a result of the defence of its interests and of its class struggle against the ruling class; a set of values which arises from the truce which is reached in this class struggle and which centres around the ideas of full employment and the welfare state; and a more generalised set of status values which grows around the margins of the value-system of the truce and which serves on a subjective level to transmute class attitudes. It is necessary for us to look at all of these aspects of the value system since the incorporation of out-siders can only be understood as incorporation into a social and value system of this order of complexity.[6]

Our criticism of the looser formulations of functionalist stratification theory is that it takes the value system of the ruling class, and the kind of competition for rewards which that value system posits, as though this were the value system of the society

6. See also T. H. Marshall, *Citizenship and Social Class*, Cambridge, 1950; and the application of Marshall's concept of 'Citizenship' to the problems of immigrant minorities in E. J. Rose, *Colour and Citizenship*, Institute of Race Relations Oxford, 1969.

as a whole. Such an approach does carry a certain amount of conviction for two reasons. One is that ruling class control of ideological institutions does mean that some of those whom they rule accept their values. This is the phenomenon of the deferential worker which has been so well described by Lockwood.[7] The other factor is that, even amongst those who do not themselves accept ruling class values as valid, there may be some recognition of the fact that they do to some extent 'hold sway'. That is to say, while it is not possible to get an entirely agreed system of social rankings when the question put is 'What do *you* think is the merited prestige of this individual or this occupation?' agreement may nonetheless be possible when the question put begins 'What do you think that other people think?'[8]

Even then, however, it is worth noticing that the notion of 'ruling class values' is a complex one. Those who actually wield economic or political power in a society are quite regularly seen as *parvenus,* whose behaviour is uncouth and contemptible, compared with that of the ruling class which existed in earlier times. This is always the case, where an industrial order has been preceded by a feudal order of some kind and, even in the case of the United States which has no such feudal past, we find that at a local community level the modern rational-capitalist industrialists are contrasted unfavourably with the families which made their money in more traditional industries. This is very clear in the case of the Yankee City studies.[9] It would seem therefore that the functionalist theory does not even explain ruling-class values, for, apart from the question of the functional importance of rôles, actions and people, a very important factor taken into consideration in ongoing value

7. D. Lockwood, 'Sources of Variation in Working Class Images of Society', *The Sociological Review,* Vol. XIV, No. 3, 1966.

8. R. Turner, 'Life Situation and Sub-Culture, A Comparison of Merited Prestige Judgements by Three Occupational Classes in Britain', *British Journal of Sociology,* Vol. VIII, 1957.

9. W. Lloyd Warner and P. Lunt, *The Social Life of a Modern Community,* Yale University Press, New Haven, Connecticut, 1941.

systems is that of legitimacy, and, particularly the kind of legitimacy which is conferred by long tradition.

In the 'lower reaches of the structure' what we have in all advanced capitalist societies, but particularly in North West Europe, is the emergence of working class culture, confusedly part-revolutionary and part defensive in its aims. It is too much to suggest that such a culture offers an institutional order which is a real alternative to that proposed by the ruling class, as Marx seems to be doing when he speaks of the political economy of the working class,[10] or when he speaks of a similar movement going on among the working class as went on amongst the bourgeoisie when it moved towards imposing its economic and political sway over the whole of society. But, short of this, it must be clear to anyone with even the most marginal political experience of European society that the defensive values of working-class society are extremely important in shaping attitudes diametrically opposed to those which the ruling class posits as normal. Indeed, anyone who has lived within a working-class community must find it a little quaint and naïve for Parsons and Merton to describe the basic security and solidarity oriented attitudes of working class culture analysed by Parsons and by Merton as a form of deviance.[11] Quite clearly, if the value order of a society was based solely upon the kind of competitive game which Merton describes, *anomie* would be inevitable. Another way of beginning, however, is simply to say that the social structure and value order is more complex than Merton's model suggests.

The third aspect of modern value systems is that which arises from the kind of solution of political problems posited by Lipset. If it is the case that working class attitudes cease to be based upon ideological politics (i.e. upon proposals to overthrow the existing order) then one would expect working class organisations and ruling class organisations alike to become

10. K. Marx and F. Engels, 'The Communist Manifesto'.
11. T. Parsons, *The Social System*, Chapter 7; R. K. Merton, *Social Theory and Social Structure*, Free Press, Glencoe, 1964, Chapter 4.

committed to certain agreed ways of dividing up social rewards and in particular to the notions of the welfare state, 'responsible' trades unionism and full employment. It goes without saying that the two sides to such an agreement will exploit these notions to give legitimacy to their own class-interests but, with this said, we have surely to admit that there is an area of agreement about the institutions of the truce,[12] and that people of all classes come to develop some moral identification with their maintenance.

The importance of stressing this third aspect of the value system and the stratification system of advanced capitalist countries, however, is that it shows how precarious any concept of agreed values really is. What we are saying, in effect, is that, so long as there is an internal balance of power within the society, an agreed set of basic politico-economic institutions is possible. If, however, the balance of power were upset by economic crisis or revolution, a quite different set of factors would begin to operate. One might revert to assertions of the ruling class value system; revolutionary ideologies might be revived; or the agreed interpretation of the total social order might be maintained only by the identification of a common enemy alleged to be threatening the system.

Finally we have to notice that, in so far as relative social peace and relative peace between the classes is achieved, it becomes increasingly difficult to maintain class organisations in fighting trim or class ideologies at the appropriate pitch necessary for the pursuit of conflict. The working classes come to see themselves and their culture as a way of life within an overall accepted social order. Instead of classes, we begin to see the emergence of a series of stratified ways of life. Such a way of looking at things always exists to some extent so long as there is the possibility of 'promotion' of members of lower groups or their children. It becomes stabilised and legitimated, however, in so far as it can be rationalised in terms of the values of the truce.

This new kind of status order is subjectively understood in terms of three main images of the total society. These we may

12. Rex, *Key Problems of Sociological Theory*, loc. cit.

describe as the image of the occupational structure, the image of the community structure and the image of the educational and power structure. We should now say something about each of these, since when we turn to the question of the rôle of minorities we shall see that a very important question is that of the objective and subjective placing of the minority group in terms of these three structures.

The occupational structure, perhaps, needs the least comment, since it has received the most exhaustive discussion in sociological literature. It will suffice to say that it has been possible in many countries, not merely to achieve broad overall classifications in terms of manual and non-manual categories or in terms of skill, but also to place individual occupations specified in meticulous detail in terms of their grading on an occupational status scale. Partly this has been done in terms of qualified acceptance of ruling class values of the 'What do you think that other people think?' type. Partly it refers to a fairly widely agreed status rating of occupations in a stable capitalist industrial system. What is perhaps most interesting as a theme for further theoretical development here is simply whether there are certain occupations which have to be rated in terms of quite different criteria than those on which the main scale is based.

One feature of the occupational status order which should be noted is that it is inherently unstable, because of its close relation to the collective bargaining process. Thus a man may think in terms of the occupational order when he considers his children's educational careers. But at work, when he is forced to negotiate over wages and conditions, his thinking will be based upon the absolute rights of the group in which he is a member. This close relationship does not exist, however, in the world of urban community, and we may expect that women, men divorced from their occupational rôles, and those who don't fit easily into the overall occupational structure, are more likely to see the stratification system in terms of stratified neighbourhoods, housing and the consumer patterns which go with different neighbourhoods and housing.

A very large part, and an increasingly large part, of men's time and emotional energy in modern society is clearly concentrated not in occupational contexts, which for many will be thought of solely in terms of disutility, but in community contexts. Increasingly, moreover, the neighbourhood in which a man lives is not exactly determined by what his occupation is or who his employer is. Thus the picture of the world which preoccupies men for a lot of the time, and housewives nearly all the time, is that of the kind of community neighbourhood they live in. 'How can we get a better house?', 'I'm proud (or ashamed) to be living in a neighbourhood like this' – these are quite central reflections and observations on the nature of society and one's place in it to be found amongst urban men. Hence the status system which Warner and his colleagues spelt out in Yankee City, is elaborated in an ecological form in the urban maps which Park and Burgess[13] and others taught sociologists to collect.

Related both to the community structure and to the occupational structure is the educational system, through which amongst other things people seek to gain access to the higher occupations, to positions of power and to community contexts of the most prestigious kinds. It is, however, worth mentioning that this educational structure does seem to be thought of as having independent significance as something to be argued about, apart from the questions of occupational and community status systems. An open educational system may be the one means through which occupational and status mobility is possible, and the degree of its openness may be one of the defining features of a social system for its participant actors and those who seek to enter it from outside.

With this overall discussion of the stratification systems of relatively stable advanced capitalist society in mind, it is now possible to turn to the question of the relationship of minorities to such system. And perhaps the first thing which we have to say is that our discussion of the stratification system helps to throw

13. R. Park and E. Burgess, *The City*, University of Chicago Press, 1967.

light on the difficult theoretical problem of defining what we mean by a minority. The paradox of many definitions such as those which we considered in our first chapter is that they seemed to say that a numerical majority might be a minority,[14] the crucial factor being the position of the group within the political order. We may now say that, while the political order is undoubtedly important, minority status in a stable and advanced capitalist society is something which is accorded to an identifiable group, which cannot readily be placed in the overall stratification system of the society.

Warner explicitly discusses the question of the ethnic groups and the status system but concentrates very largely on the assimilation of ethnic minorities of European origin. What emerges therefore, is a picture of some group, like the Poles, undergoing a twofold process of acculturation and social mobility. At the outset such minorities enter the lower reaches of the structure, though how low the point of entry might depend upon the evaluation of the national group in terms of some international scale of status comparisons. As they change culturally, however, so they advance up the status scale. Thus 'lace-curtain Irish' are still recognisable Irish, but can occupy a higher status position than the last newcomers. Finally the problem of placing the ethnic minorities disappears, because they are no longer identifiable as an ethnic minority.

Further development of the theory of minorities and of race relations in advanced capitalist societies must involve the modification of Warner's model in two directions. On the one hand recognition must be given to the complexity of the stratification system which the immigrant tries to enter. On the other, it must be recognised that different immigrant minorities have different careers as far as their relation to the 'host' stratification system is concerned.

The simplest case is that of a minority which is seen as having the right to full entry into the host country's social system. Whether this right exists and in what degree will depend upon

14. See Simpson and Yinger, *op. cit.*, Chapter 1.

historical, political and economic factors in the particular country's history. Israel presents us with a case in which being an immigrant is not merely not an undesirable characteristic, but in terms of the country's ideology is actually a prestigious one. And in the United States, where the country had to be peopled by new immigrants, and where the melting pot ideology recognised the acculturation process as a normal process in the society, some groups at least were recognised as having a right of entry and social acceptance, even though this right was not universally extended. On the other hand in the established industrial societies of Europe where immigrant populations were small in relation to the total, the immigrant was perhaps more likely to be looked on with suspicion.

Having the right of entry into the advanced society's stratification system, of course, by no means implies that the immigrant has an automatic right of entry into the society's highest status groups. In a complex and class-divided, if stable, society what is at issue is entry into the stratification system at some point. Thus the first step which an Irishman in an English city might take is that of becoming a member of the working class. Thereafter, he may make further progress in terms of status mobility but the first step of getting into the system is the most important and is different from all the others.

This problem is somewhat complicated by the fact that in many metropolitan cities one of the characteristics of the 'working class' is its cosmopolitan nature, so that it is difficult to draw the distinction we have just made. We cannot say definitively 'This man has moved from the status of being an Irish immigrant to that of being a member of the working class' because 'working-class' may be a rather Irish thing to be. This factor is, of course, particularly important in the United States but rather less so in the older industrial countries where newcomers confront a working-class population who, if they have immigrant origin at all, have to trace it back over several generations. But in every case a theoretical distinction can be drawn between the ethnically varied and cosmopolitan characteristics of ways of life within the system and those characteristics which define a man as being outside of it.

In this simplest case, where the assimilation of the minority is recognised as legitimate, difficulties and conflict between immigrant groups and their hosts are likely to last only a few generations. It is true that there will be conflict and that relations with new minorities will be governed by unfavourable myths and stereotypes, but is misleading to say, as is sometimes said by the descendants of immigrants discussing the position of negroes and Jews, that there is no difference between the position of these groups and the position of the immigrant group's own ancestors. The difference is that the unfavourably judged characteristics in the latter case were always thought of as capable of being socialised or learned away in a few generations.

What finally happens to a group of immigrants which seeks assimilation in a society in which the assimilation of that kind of group is regarded as legitimate, is that they either lose their cultural characteristics entirely or retain only symbolic token features which are not thought of by the host community as threatening or undesirable in any way. Such is the situation of Scotsmen abroad who celebrate 'Burns nicht' at meetings of Caledonian societies and it is useful to conceptualise this situation as a 'caledonian situation'.

When we go beyond talking about the structural bases underlying race relations situations to deciding which are, sociologically speaking, true race relations situations, we shall find that the kind of relationships and processes which we have been discussing thus far rarely if ever lead to true race relations problems. This is not the case, however, if a minority group seeks to attain a non-assimilated and distinct position in a society which encourages or demands assimilation; nor is it the case where minorities seek either to secede from or to dominate the society of their hosts.

Groups which seek to maintain their cultural separateness permanently are in fact rare. Most alleged cases of this kind turn out on further investigation to be of other types. They may refer to caledonian situations; they may be cases in which the separateness of the minority is, in fact, imposed on it by a group, which then rationalises its action, by claiming that this is what the segregated groups want; they may be cases of short-term migration of a group, few of whose members intend to remain permanently; or they may refer to a phase in the career of assimilation of a minority which appears separate for the moment, but which will be assimilated within a generation or so.

There are, however, some genuine cases of groups which do not seek assimilation. Usually there is some religious factor involved in their choice. Thus both Jewish and Muslim immigrants in industrial societies find it important to maintain their identity and require separate or supplementary educational facilities and places of worship, as well as supplies of food appropriate to their religious practice. It is conceivable that the demands which such a group makes are so limited, or that the host society is relatively so tolerant of intergroup difference, that this appears as hardly different from a caledonian situation. But very often there is a conflict between the group's desire for distinction and the insistence upon the elimination of alien cultural practices by their hosts.

Unfortunately history does not always present us with all the crucial cases which we should like for comparative scientific reasoning. If it did we should like to know whether the situation in which a distinct identity is sought but not permitted ever existed in circumstances in which the religious and ethnic minority did not have the position of a pariah group in the host society. In fact in the case of the Jews, the cases which we can discover in the advanced capitalist countries tend to be either of a relatively mild caledonian variety or they are cases in which there is some degree of occupational specialisation in what is regarded as an ethically dubious sphere of economic activity. All that we can say then, is that as compared with most European groups migrating to another European country or to the United States, Jewish minorities have been distinguished by a determination to maintain their identity and sometimes by a noticeable degree of occupational specialisation.

An immigrant group which sought to secede from the society to which its members had deliberately come would be a contradiction in terms. But the goal of secession has been adopted by minorities in a number of European countries. Usually it turns out that the group concerned feels that it is not being allowed assimilation, or that it is being discriminated against, and minorities of this kind serve to draw our attention also to the pluralism of many European countries. Thus just as minorities have been forced to accept an inferior position in colonial societies in Africa, Asia and Latin America, so also in the creation and recreation of national states in Europe, there have emerged national minorities with a sense of their own deprivation and a desire to achieve an independent existence. There is a possibility that this sort of situation represented in the conflicts engendered by minority nationalisms in Europe might take the form of race relations problems.

Finally, amongst situations created by the migration and settlement of European minorities, we should notice those cases in which a minority seeks neither assimilation in nor secession from the social system of the country where it settles, but seeks instead to dominate that country. In the United States the issue never arose in a serious form since, after the suppression of the Indians the right of the English immigrants to impose their culture and way of life was undisputed. In the case of Israel on the other hand, the immigrants succeeded in establishing their own social order in a country where the majority of the population had been Arabs. And in South Africa and in Canada minorities of European ancestry who had not originally been in a position of political power sought to capture it and, if not actually dominating the society and imposing its own cultural order, at least achieving a shared ruling status based upon the maintenance of bilingualism and cultural diversity.

Whatever the desires of the group, and whatever the reaction to it of the host society, there will be at least a period in which some degree of separation from the host society is evident. Thus the group might be confined to relatively menial jobs and to certain overcrowded rooming house areas in the city. As we shall see in a moment it may be difficult to differentiate in practice between the transitory cases in which all this happens as a phase in the minority's assimilation and cases where segregation is enforced against its will. We should wish to emphasise here, however, that even when there is no element of deliberate coercion involved, some kind of colony structure emerges amongst the minority group. This is a set of organisations and groups, or, more generally a network of social relations based upon the group's original culture, through which first and second generation immigrants find a degree of social, economic and psychological security, until they or their children are in a position to live securely within the wider social structure of the host society. Such colonies may be very visible; they may involve a considerable measure of segregation and they might involve the living in close proximity of groups which are permitted to assimilate and groups which are not. Nonetheless, it is important to notice that the existence of colony structures does not imply all that is involved in the term 'ghetto'. What we are calling a colony here is a temporary grouping of immigrants which can act as a spring-board for entry into the host society. By definition this is never true of the ghetto.

We must now turn to another and quite distinct aspect of minority problems in metropolitan capitalist countries. In talking about the Jews above, we noted that the maintenance of their distinct identity might result from a real or imagined specialisation in ethically dubious occupations. We had also noticed that in colonial societies certain groups seemed to be in the position of pariah castes. We should now notice that, although in so many respects the social structure of the metropolitan capitalist countries is different from colonial societies, in one respect they are similar. In both cases there are certain occupations which, although essential to the functioning of the society or economy, are considered to be morally dubious in the society's value system. Thus, just as the alien traders who seek profit in traditional colonial society are regarded with suspicion, so also the more openly usurious forms of moneylending, land-lordism and 'sweating' are objects of suspicion in metropolitan society. Such rôles are conveniently left to outsiders who can be blamed and punished for carrying out their essential tasks.

The value system in terms of which such judgments are made has complex origins and a complex structure. In the first place it should be noted that it is located in the most legitimate 'feudal' part of the ruling class value system. Such judgments have a history going back to the mediaeval church's denunci-ation of the man who was a 'taker of advantages'. But similar values are also embodied both in the working class counter-culture and what we have called the value system of the truce. Of course, the more stable the welfare system of the society, the less scope and need there will be for this kind of alien minority, but there have been few societies which have dispensed with the need for groups in this position.

Apart from being a pariah group attached to the stratified but stable society an alien minority in this position might also serve as a scapegoat. As we have seen, both the value system of the truce and the parvenu element of the ruling class value system are highly unstable, and could very readily lose the support of large sections of the population. Hence the existence of an alien group which can act as an alternative target for popular resentment is a very important sociological mechanism for maintaining a precarious evaluative and social order.

The groups which we have been discussing here are, of course, in a quite different sociological position from those which we discussed earlier. They do not necessarily enter the strati-fication system from the bottom. They are better thought of as attached to it half way up, but essentially as remaining morally outside of the society. Their problems as a minority are quite different from those of working class minorities and it is in fact surprising that patterns of social relations such as they have with the society at large should have been subject to the same kind of racist rationalisation as the relation of working-class immigrants to their society. It is therefore necessary to draw attention to the fact that so far as metropolitan capitalist societies are concerned there are two main sorts of 'race relations' problems. One consists of relations between groups of manual workers of alien and often of colonial origin and the host society. The other is concerned with the rôle of pariah and scapegoat groups performing some kind of commercial functions.

There is one point which should be made here in order that we should not be misunderstood. We are not implying that Jews in Europe or America, Lebanese in West Africa, or Indians in East Africa do in fact work solely in occupations which are objectively morally dubious. The judgment about moral dubiousness as well as the judgment about the demographic facts to which we refer are simply the judgments of other groups in the society. But there is one especial point we should make, in addition, which casts some doubt on the absoluteness of the distinction made in the last paragraph. Jews in England have been thought of as successful businessmen, even when they included a very large minority of working class tailors, and Indians in South Africa are thought of as storekeepers, although most of them originated as, and some still are, labourers on sugar plantations. What we are saying when we talk of two kinds of structures is really a statement about two different stereotypes in terms of which the members of metropolitan societies organise their thinking about minorities.

When we were speaking of European minorities before, we spoke as though they all had equal possibilities of assimilation. We should now note that this is only relatively true. A great deal depends upon the history and social structure of the country from which the immigrants come and the way in which that history and social structure is perceived by people in the host society. If the immigrants are thought of as coming from a society in which on average the range of occupational and other social rôles is much the same as in the host country, the chance of assimilation will be maximised. If they are peasants coming to an urban society, their chances may be less. If they are an unknown quantity, or if they come from an underdeveloped country, their chances of assimilation may be least of all.

One kind of immigrant, however, presents quite peculiar problems. This is the immigrant from the colonial territories. His assimilation is clearly going to depend upon the kind of rôle which members of the host society normally assign to the colonial worker and the possibility of a man who is thought of as having such a rôle being able to enter the stratification system of the metropolitan society. This is clearly the case when we are dealing with immigrants from colonial territories to metropolitan European countries, but it is also true of American negroes migrating from the economy and society of the Deep South to the Northern cities.

In fact the value system of the metropolitan societies, and the consequent stratification system which we described, makes no reference in itself to colonial rôles and statuses, and it is important now to look at what is implicit in it and what must be added to it in order that it should be used as a factor in explaining reactions to the arrival of the colonial worker.

We have from time to time suggested that the stratification system of a society arises from the subjective picture or model of social relations which comes to men's minds when they think of their society as a whole. It is sometimes convenient in this regard to put bounds about the society and to ask simply what picture men have of the system of social relations within the metropolitan nation. But equally, it is sometimes useful to look at a wider picture which takes in not merely social relations within the metropolitan country, but within the whole imperial and colonial system. Indeed we must do this if we are to understand the position of the colonial worker who migrates to the metropolitan country.

We might, if we wished, speak of a *stratification* system which covered not merely a single metropolitan country, but a worldwide empire. This is a matter of terminology. We should have to recognise, however, that any scale which was suggested as the basis for grading the various groups, strata, social segments and individuals was, to say the least of it, multi-dimensional. Perhaps, therefore, what is most important from our point of view is that we should suggest what elements in the metropolitan citizen's perception of the colonial immigrant are most significant in mapping his place in relation to the metropolitan stratification structure. What seem to us to be most important are the political and economic status of the colonial worker, as it is understood, his stage in cultural evolution and his colour and other physical characteristics.

Of some importance here is the source of information about the colonial worker. We suggest that the most common source and point of reference is the picture given by individual informants who have participated in some capacity in colonial society, whether as colonial officials, managers and overseers of productive establishments, settlers, soldiers or missionaries. Such direct evidence may be confirmed and rationalised by the mass media, but it is important to remember that individuals do have this contact through personal networks. There can have been few families in Victorian Britain who did not have at least one member who had participated in some capacity or other in colonial society, and, even in the period after 1945, as former colonies gained independence, there were few European countries which were not involved for long periods in direct colonial wars, or in policing duties following civil wars.

As we pointed out in our discussion of colonial society it is of the essence of colonial labour relations that they are based upon force. Since most metropolitan families were in contact with someone who at some stage will have participated in the use of that force, the stereotype of colonial people in general, which is likely to survive in metropolitan thinking, is that of the colonial man as a 'savage' or a 'terrorist'. On the other hand, if the experience which was vouchsafed to a particular family's representative is a peaceful one, it is still likely to be an experience of the colonial worker as an unfree worker. In either case his position appears as being in stark contrast to any of the possible positions within the metropolitan status system. Whatever else may be said of a free metropolitan worker, his position cannot be based upon the same degree of coercion, as is thought of as normal for the colonial worker. Thus, from the point of view of ruling class values, of the counter-value system of the metropolitan working class, or the value system of the truce, the colonial man is a man who stands outside the stratified set of positions in normal society. He is beneath the bottom of the stratification system, and the problem therefore is whether he is to have his status altered, or if the system is to be extended and made more complex to take account of other factors.

It should be noted that this problem is not lessened if one takes account of other aspects of the image and stereotype of the colonial man than those relating to his military defeat and his coercion as a worker. The missionary, the monarch or politician going out to receive some kind of feudal homage from colonial tributary, even the idealistic young student going out on 'voluntary service overseas' brings back an image of an inferior person underdeveloped and backward, even if meriting aid from the developed countries.

Given these facts the colonial immigrant would in any case start at a disadvantage, on entering metropolitan society and competing with other kinds of immigrants. Thus one would expect him to be at a disadvantage in Paris, as much as in Chicago or Birmingham. But there is nonetheless a greater possibility that the colonial immigrant will be recognised as capable of attaining the status of some kind of free worker and thus entering the stratification system, if colour and other physical characteristics are not taken as a sign of status. It does seem to be the case that, in the Protestant countries, an absolute distinction is maintained between white men and any kind of black or coloured man, whereas in the Catholic countries colour as such has little classificatory importance. Hence the principal problem is what happens to the coloured worker in those countries which use skin colour as a means of discriminating between men.

What seems to happen is that colour is taken as the indication that a man is only entitled to colonial status, and this means that he has to be placed outside the normal stratification system. The stratification system thus becomes extended to take account of additional social positions marked by a degree of rightlessness not to be found amongst the incorporated workers.

There are, in any case, certain rôles and positions within metropolitan society which are an embarrassment in terms of its professed ideals. In all the advanced countries it has been observed that there are new groups of poor and underprivileged people, for whom neither the welfare system, nor economic affluence, nor trade union bargaining adequately provide. Those in the more backward sections of the productive system suffer relative deprivation compared with their fellow-workers who have benefited from technological advance, and, even if their own industries did undergo technological change, it might well be that they would simply become permanently unemployed. Similarly technological advance implies an educated labour force, and some citizens will lack sufficient education to be able to obtain one of the fewer jobs available. And, jobs apart, whatever a man's income, it appears that certain important social benefits like housing cannot be accorded to all members of the population, but only to those who have certain characteristics. Thus, when the colonial worker enters metropolitan society, he finds, not merely that there is a disinclination to treat him as a citizen, as belonging within the normal stratification system. He finds that there are a number of ill-defined new poor rôles waiting for him. If it is accepted in the particular metropolitan society that colour is a relevant discriminating index, his classification is likely to be even more automatic.

So far as occupation is concerned, the colonial worker first finds acceptance as a replacement worker. He finds that there are certain jobs not yet eliminated by technical advance which are so arduous or unpleasant that they are not acceptable to the majority of the metropolitan working class. And he finds when he seeks to house himself that there are certain kinds of house occupancy which are least desired by the metropolitan population which are the only types available to him.[15]

With this much said, however, it might be argued that the colonial immigrant is in no different position from any other immigrant. This is where all poor immigrant workers start. What happens, however, is that the colonial worker's position is doubly differentiated. First, he is more severely confined to the position of replacement worker and resident, and second and most important, he cannot expect with confidence that his children or grandchildren will have been accepted into the stratification system of the host society.

Clearly the coloured colonial worker in Britain or the negro immigrant to the Northern American cities is not a man who is simply living temporarily in the urban immigrant colony. In the second generation his children find that there is no way out and up for them. It is not quite true to say that they will necessarily live in a ghetto, for they will not be entirely cut off from people of different ethnic backgrounds. But what will be true is that the places where they live and work and the people amongst whom they live and work will not be covered by the value system of the society as a whole. Physically they live within the society. Morally they remain outside of it.[16]

One feature of the colonial worker's situation he does share with immigrants who occupy commercial rôles. This is that, being outside of the society, he may also be treated as a scapegoat to be blamed for its failures. Thus the evils of unemployment or bad housing can be blamed on coloured immigrants flooding into the country and overtaxing the social service, just as easily as they can on Jewish moneylenders and landlords. In either case the solidarity of the social order in its post-political phase can be maintained by directing resentment against the out-group. The difference between the two kinds of group lies

15. Political and Economic Planning, *Report of Racial Discrimination*, London, 1968; J. Rex and R. Moore, *Race, Community and Conflict*, Oxford, 1967.

16. J. Rex, 'The Sociology of a Zone of Transition', in R. Pahl, *Readings in Urban Sociology*, Pergamon, London, 1968, pp. 211–31.

simply in the fact that, whereas the commercial groups are thought of as only being outside the stratification system, the colonial workers are thought of as being beneath it.

Where colour is not recognised as having classificatory significance, as in France, there remains the fact that some immigrants to French metropolitan society are nonetheless known to be colonial workers. To the extent that they are, we should expect that similar considerations to those we have previously discussed would apply, and there is indeed some evidence that first Algerian workers, and then those from Guadeloupe and Martinique and the associated states in Africa have been discriminated against, and have not been fully accepted into the French class and stratification system. Nonetheless it is an important fact that, where colour is not taken to be an absolutely reliable indicator of colonial status, there is more possibility of assimilation into the system. Thus one finds that in French hotels the mere presence of a coloured man does not create the same feeling of tension and unease that it is likely to do in England. This is, however, quite compatible with the existence of prejudice and discrimination being directed against immigrant workers from overseas territories.

An alternative explanation of the different experience of coloured people in French and English society might be offered, which made no reference to colonialism at all. According to this view, the value system of British society includes the notion of the inferiority of coloured people, whereas the French system does not. Too little comparative work has been done for us to decide between this theory and our own. What we are advancing ourselves, however, is itself a very moderate position. We do not say that colour discrimination rests solely and completely on an appreciation of the colonial status of the coloured worker. What we are saying is that, where colour discrimination is consistent with the metropolitan culture and value system, it is likely to operate as a means of classifying the colonial immigrant, and placing him in a state of relative rightlessness outside the stratification order.

One further problem remains. This is that, since all immigrant minorities have begun by being outside the stratification system, and have succeeded in becoming incorporated into it, it has to be shown that this destiny is not likely to be available to coloured colonial immigrants. In order to show this we need to look at American experience where the distinction between the absorption of, say, the Irish or Italian minority has features quite different from that of the American negro and Puerto Rican minorities.

It is important to begin here by noticing that the various European minorities have not been incorporated into American society through general goodwill on the part of the host society permitting individual immigrants to become Americanised. Their incorporation has depended upon political mechanisms such as the spoils system which have made worthwhile a political transaction between those who direct the political machines and the leaders of the immigrant group concerned. What we have to do is to see the similarities and the differences between the deployment of immigrant power by these groups on the one hand, and the growth of the Black Power ideology and movement on the other.

In the case of the Italians, their social segregation in the first generation meant that they maintained a fairly tight colony structure, which recognised particular members as political leaders. In the absence of a well established native working class movement, political parties seeking working class support were dependent to a peculiar degree on the support of these immigrant leaders. Not merely therefore did these leaders enter into relations with the political bosses from a position of strength. Some of them became bosses themselves. There could be no clearer way of entering the stratification system. Once entry had been achieved, then, in the United States as in other countries, the children of those who formed the working class political machine were likely to find their way up the stratification ladder.

It has sometimes been suggested naïvely and hopefully that the Black Power movement is simply based upon a proposal that negroes should enter into a similar relationship with the system. Such a theory, however, will not stand up unless it can be supported by some subsidiary hypothesis which explains why the incorporation of the negro has not already occurred. The negro community has been there, its leaders and the political bosses have been there, but the transaction has not taken place, or at least has not taken place to anything like the same extent as it has done with other minorities.

But even if we leave open the possibility that America's international position or some other factor imposes on its government a new commitment to interracial equality and that the door is therefore opened for incorporation of coloured minorities we should still need to look at alternative lines of development in any comprehensive study of minorities and race relations in metropolitan societies. What, therefore, are the other possibilities available to the Black Power movement.

The ideologists of the movement quite clearly see themselves as planning a revolution. They deny the moral authority of the social system in which they live, making this quite clear by referring to all whites inclusively as 'pigs'. They refuse to accept the now traditional depreciation of negro qualities which has given the negro a white ego-ideal, and they assert, as forcefully and repetitively as possible, that 'Black is beautiful'. They devote themselves to instilling these ideas into the young, and they openly support the use of violence to defend negro rights in white society.

In a very important way this set of strategies is revolutionary. Instead of the negro banging on the doors of white society, pleading to get his foot on the white stratification ladder, he rejects the stratification system and the moral order on which it rests, and talks of black separatism. But this is not a revolutionary ideology, in the sense of proposing the overthrow of the existing order and the establishment of a negro dominated one. In the long term the negro revolution must surely lead either to secession by the negroes, to some kind of incorporation, or to permanent and sustained conflict.

Secession either in the form of emigration or of the establishment of black areas in the United States, is not a likely long-
term alternative, if only because these are strategies more
appropriate to a position of weakness, whereas the negro's
position is one of increasing strength. What therefore is likely to
happen is that although he has been denied admission to the
political and the stratification systems by the normal democratic
channels, he may be successful in shooting his way in. But, if the
urban riots do not lead to this outcome, there remains only the
possibility of the rioting continuing.

Another aspect of the American negro situation which
deserves consideration is the relationship between the negro
revolt and the situation of the poor and underprivileged who are
not coloured. It has been suggested that the location of the
negroes and their revolt amongst the new poor might mean that
the latter have an opportunity in America, which they lack
elsewhere, of finding in a negro-led civil rights movement a
political means of self-defence or even of 'incorporation'. There
may be something in this, in that it is negro militancy which has
been the main source of pressure which has led to anti-poverty
programmes. It is significant, however, that this view of the
future is held only by 'white liberals', negro moderates, and
Marxists. The likelihood still seems to be that the negro revolt
will continue independently and will pursue its own goals.

The revolt of the American negro is in many respects something of a special case, for the American negro is far more a part
of the cultural and social system of the country in which he lives
than are coloured minorities in other metropolitan countries.
The possibility of political incorporation by peaceful or non-
peaceful means seems to be less in other countries such as
England which share the colour attitudes of the United States,
rather than Spain or Portugal or France. Nonetheless one
feature of the English situation is likely to be that its coloured
minorities will begin to talk in terms of Black Power if only
through the diffusion of political ideologies from the United
States.

In the English case, and indeed in the French case, it is too early to do more than speculate about possible outcomes, for the phenomenon of relatively large-scale immigration of coloured workers from the former plantation colonies is a relatively new one. All the firm evidence we have is of a first generation group of immigrants. Such immigrants may be temporary and may be content to remain unassimilated, or they may be content to live in the security of the immigrant colony for a generation. The question is whether their children would be allowed the possibility of assimilation or incorporation and, if not, what would happen. At that point a lot would depend upon numbers and upon relative power. The development of a permanent posture of militant self-defence is the most likely outcome if numbers are small. Otherwise alternatives similar to those in the United States would open up.

All that has been said here assumes, of course, that the question of minorities remains divorced from the problems of international relations. In the long term, however, it may not, and when American negro leaders in the nineteen-sixties talked of creating another Vietnam in the United States, they were drawing attention to the vulnerability of American society domestically as well as internationally. From our point of view we should ask of the metropolitan societies whether they are viable entities, given that they have unincorporated colonial minorities, just as surely as we should ask whether Malaysia or Guyana is viable given its pluralism.

Our aim, however, is not to predict the future. What we have been doing here is to review the variety of types of intergroup structure which exist in metropolitan society just as in previous chapters we were concerned with a typology of productive and social systems in colonial countries. We must now consider how far the kinds of situations which we have been discussing constitute race relations situations. This will mean first looking at the degree to which the treatment accorded to a group depends upon ascriptive criteria so that transfer from one group to another is restricted, and second, looking at the kinds of belief system which rationalise and sustain and legitimise such a system. We shall argue that the patterns of intergroup relations which we have discussed here are of the kind which are necessary for the emergence of race relations problems. They are not, however, to be thought of as a sufficient condition for the emergence of these problems. Patterns of intergroup discrimination and beliefs make a difference to what occurs and part of the understanding of race relations lies in understanding them.

5. Discrimination, Exploitation, Oppression and Racialism

The conceptualisation of the field of study which is the sociology of race relations is clearly a difficult process. So far we have been concerned only with the kind of situations in which a race relations problem may emerge. But none of these situations is by itself a race relations situation. It is possible to have the varying degrees of freedom and unfreedom which we described in Chapter Two without the problem of labour relations being defined as a racial one. It might be possible to have a situation in which conquerors and conquered retain their separate identities and live side by side without the notion of racial difference being raised. And it might be possible to have categories of people left out of the incorporated stratification system fo metropolitan societies without this group being considered as racially distinct.

Any of these situations, however, might develop into a race relations situation, and some situation of the kinds mentioned would seem to be a precondition of the emergence of a racial problem. What is necessary to complete the process whereby such a problem emerges is firstly that there should be a certain kind of practice in the treatment of the members of a group, and, secondly, that there should be a certain kind of theoretical definition of the situation. In this chapter we shall try to deal with the first of these.

So far as the element of practice is concerned, what we have in mind is that whenever there is a race relations situation, one of its features is that all members of a group are regarded by virtue of possessing certain recognisable characteristics of that group, as being entitled to certain defined rights or as being assigned to certain defined rôles. This would seem to distinguish such situations from the overlapping category of stratification situations in which some possibility exists that, despite his observable characteristics, an individual might move from one category to another. We might say, therefore, that it is essential to a race relations situation as we define it, that there should be a restriction on social mobility, or, to use the fashionable Parsonian jargon, that rôles in such a situation are ascribed rather than achieved.[1]

It will be pointed out, of course, that ascriptive rôle allocation or the existence of a barrier to mobility is a characteristic of certain kinds of stratification situations, and that this is one of the principal dimensions in terms of which stratification systems may be compared. With this we would certainly agree. Indeed, we would argue that wherever a stratification system has this feature, it might develop in a race relations direction. For this very reason we are not surprised that one of the classic ways of conceptualising the problem of negro-white relations in America has been in terms of an incipient caste system. There clearly is an overlap. But we would also want to point out that there might be situations in which, while conceptualisation in terms of caste seems inappropriate, the factor of ascriptive rôle allocation is nonetheless present. We therefore see ascriptive rôle allocation as the essential second element in race relations, and not the more specific factor of caste.

We could, of course, avoid speaking in this theoretically rather laboured way, if we were simply to say that the feature which differentiated the field of race relations from the wider study of social structure and social stratification was that the criteria of differentiation in race relations were derived from certain kinds of popularly held theories. This we shall not say, however, for several important reasons.

In the first place, we wish to reject the oversimplification which says that the practice of racialism is something which follows

1. Parsons, *The Social System*, p. 67.

from belief in racist theories. This, it seems to us, implies a commitment to a unidirectional view of the relations between ideas and social action and social structure which cannot be justified. Secondly we believe that there may be situations in which a practice emerges which is not supported by any kind of explicit theory. And lastly there may well be cases in which a practice continues after its theoretical justifications have become disreputable and have been abandoned.

The point we are making here appears to be in accordance with Talcott Parsons' approach to the analysis of social systems. It will be noted there that the existence of the basic pattern variables and their usefulness in sociological analysis is seen as something independent of the society's belief systems. We are arguing in fact that one of the variables (ascription/achievement) is essential to analysing the differences between racial and non-racial situations in sociology.

We do not, however, wish to go to the other extreme from that represented by the theory which says that racism is the cause of racialism, and say that racist theories are a mere epiphenomenon caused by basic forms of exploitation, oppression and discrimination, or at least put forward by a ruling class to justify its position. This is sometimes offered as a Marxist explanation of the emergence of a racial problem. Our own view is that the element of ascriptive rôle allocation is an intermediate term between factors such as class conflict and exploitation on the one hand, and racist theories on the other. At the least we should note that it is always a feature of a race relations structure that it is one *group* which exploits another and not just individual rôle players. Equally we should argue that racist theories always explain group rather than individual differences.

Another way of oversimplifying the position would be to say that it is always a feature of race relations situations that discrimination or rôle-allocation is made in terms of criteria based upon physical appearance. This is a particularly common view at the present time when the most pressing race relations problems have to do with the differences between black and white. We do, however, wish to keep open the possibility of treating relations between groups which are not physically distinguishable in the same frame of reference in terms of which we look at black-white relations. We do this, partly because of the important case of European anti-semitism, whose similarities with other racial problems far outweigh the differences, and partly because we believe that there are a number of cases where groups distinguished by differences of culture or religion interact in ways very similar to black and white groups.

In saying this we are not seeking to expand the field of the sociology of race relations so as to include all relations between ethnically distinct groups. It is perfectly possible to recognise that there is much in common between one situation and another in terms of the pattern of rôle allocation, and still to say that, within this larger category of situations, a narrower category may be distinguished on other groups. But what we are saying is that this narrower category might include some situations in which physical differences like colour are not important, while it might exclude some situations in which they are. Thus it is conceivable that we might see the problem of relations between Protestant and Roman Catholic in Northern Ireland as more central to the study of race relations than the study of relations between black and white in Paris or Lisbon. The former situation would be of interest to us if apart from discrimination against Roman Catholics as a group, it also appeared that there was conflict on the structural level and that the discrimination was supported by theories as to the sorts of behaviour and characteristics which followed inevitably from being a Catholic.[2]

The problem of which situations are to be included and which excluded from the field of race relations is a complex one. Our own position might be represented diagrammatically as follows:

2. Recently a civil rights worker in Northern Ireland, for example, claimed that 'a man's politics in N. Ireland were determined by the baptismal water'.

	High degree of consensus between strata or segments		High degree of conflict between strata or segments	
Pattern of role allocation	1	2	3	4
Ascriptive	Supported by racist theory	Not supported by racist theory	Supported by racist theory	Not supported by racist theory
Achievement oriented	Notion of racist theory inapplicable here			
	5	6	7	8

Our view is that Boxes 3 and 4 are of concern to the student of race relations, but that if the field is to be strictly and narrowly defined, we should say that only 3 falls strictly within the field. A lot of course, depends here on what we include under the heading of racist theory. This is something to be dealt with in the next chapter. Here, however, we might make it clear that, if racist theory is regarded as narrowly confined to explicit theories about intergroup genetic difference, we should have to say that we insisted on keeping Box 4 under review. If, however, racist theories are more inclusively defined to include other kinds of theory apart from genetic ones, and if theory is recognised as existing not merely on a highly rationalised and abstract level but 'in society's finger-tips', i.e. at the level at which proverbs and stereotypes affect practice, we should then find it worth while to confine the study of race relations to Box 3 only.

This chapter, of course, is concerned with the second level of differentiation of race relations studies, and so far we have described the distinctive features of the category of situations in which we are interested only on the highest level of abstraction. The question now is why we do not use language which is more commonly used in the study of race relations. Why, that is, should we speak of ascriptive rôle allocation and not simply of discrimination? Our answer to this is that the problem of discrimination is the problem of ascriptive rôle allocation as it appears only in societies having particular kinds of value system. What we have to do is to consider the way in which it occurs in a wide variety of types of society.

In the table above, we noted that a race relations situation was to be found in those cases in which there was a high degree of conflict between social strata or segments. We now have to notice that this conflict might be of several kinds. In the first place there is the kind of conflict in which a minority group is seeking to enter the stratification system from below. In the second, there is the sort of conflict which exists because two or more groups are in competition for limited resources. Thirdly, there is the situation in which punitive policies are pursued by one group against another. Fourthly, there is the situation in which one group seeks systematically to exploit the labour of another. And finally there is a situation of virtual civil war. In all of these cases, members of the society may assign each other in their own minds to specific positions and to a specific entitlement to rewards according to certain fixed and observable characteristics.

The first situation is one which has been of most concern to European and American students of race relations. In this case members of a minority group are denied the normal rights of citizenship which have been accorded even to the lowest strata in the overall social system. They, on the other hand, do not accept their exclusion, and it is for this reason that it becomes necessary from those who wish to exclude them, that they should be clearly distinguishable. So there arises a practice of discriminating against, say, Roman Catholics or coloured people which, although it may not be based upon an explicitly formulated rule, is sufficient to keep the group concerned from enjoying normal rights.

The second sort of conflict arises when two groups seek to control limited resources of some kind. This is often of very great importance, and is, indeed, one of the key variables which Wagley and Harris[3] use in classifying minority group situations. We should say that there are other types of conflict which do not

3. Wagley and Harris, *op. cit.*, p. 273.

arise from competitition of this sort, but would agree that it is useful to classify many minority group situations in metropolitan society in terms of the 'arena of competition'. This kind of competition, moreover, leads to a classical type of conflict situation (i.e. one of the type which is most commonly discussed in conflict theory). At this point, however, all that we wish to note is that, where such intergroup competitition exists, as in the other types of conflict situation mentioned, it is necessary for the competing groups to discriminate against each other if they are to preserve what they perceive to be their competitive advantages.

Different from this competitive situation is the situation in which a group has become a scapegoat and becomes the object of punitive policies pursued by dominant groups. Here again, the way in which intergroup relations are likely to develop as the punishment becomes more intense, can be analysed in formal sociological terms, but the one essential of all such scapegoating situations is that the criteria of membership of the scapegoating group should be clear so that members can instantly be recognised.

The fourth situation is one which is common in colonial contexts. What is involved is exploitation of one group by another. Here the members of the exploiting group do not compete against each other for the use of the labour services of those whom they exploit. If they were to do so, bidding for labour, by offering better conditions and greater degrees of freedom, would soon undermine the system. For the purposes of this system all of those who have certain recognisable cultural or physical characteristics are assumed to share the same degree of rightlessness. Criteria of discrimination are therefore essential.

Finally, we have the situation which exists at the foundation and during the period of break-up of a plural society. Individuals see themselves as belonging not to the society as a whole but to one of its segments. Hence there must be clear signs as to which segment an individual belongs to show whether he is of the in-group or the out-group.

What we are trying to show here is that the behaviour which one group adopts towards another may take a number of quite different forms. In popular discussion of race relations problems, however, these distinctions are rarely made. Aspects of one or other of the kinds of situation we have mentioned are taken up and generalised to cover all cases. On the 'reactionary' side of this debate are those who emphasise the notion of intergroup struggle (i.e. one fifth situation above) and claim that it has existed at all times and will continue to do so. On the 'liberal' side there are those who having observed the relatively genteel process of discrimination in advanced and stable and unitary societies, try to treat all other cases in these terms.

It is, however, clear that the term 'discrimination' is used in a number of different contexts. On the one hand, one has the case of a society in which there is some kind of ideological or institutional backing for the idea that all men, including members of minority groups, are entitled to equal rights. Here reference to discrimination refers to a kind of behaviour which is deviant in terms of the society's value system. On the other hand, we may speak of discrimination in referring to a phase in the development of a number of different types of intergroup situations. In fact such situations can only exist at all if it is possible to discriminate between one individual and another, and assign each to a particular group. In this sense of the term we might say that discrimination is at the centre of all race relations problems. But by distinguishing this usage from the one mentioned earlier, we should still be able to go on to show that there were a number of further features of race relations situations over and above 'discrimination'.

Even if we simply discuss minorities in metropolitan countries, it is clear that a greater variety of situations exist than can be summed up under the single term 'discrimination' as it is used in the narrower sense. Thus Simpson and Yinger suggest that minorities themselves will vary in the policy they pursue towards the host society and the host society may pursue a number of different policies towards them. The minorities might seek pluralistic coexistence, they might seek assimilation, they might wish to secede or they might seek to overthrow the existing order and establish their own dominance. On the other hand, the host society might pursue any one of the varieties of policy mentioned in Chapter One. They were as follows:

1. Assimilation (*a*) forced, (*b*) permitted.
2. Pluralism.
3. Legal protection of minorities.
4. Population transfer (*a*) peaceful transfer,
   (*b*) forced migration.
5. Continued subjugation.
6. Extermination.

This approach is a useful one, for it does show that, even where there is no explicit racist theory, one might have a number of situations in intergroup relations where a group is systematically, and as a matter of policy, accorded unequal rights, and in which its own wishes with regard to its relations to the society as a whole are disregarded. What we are interested in are cases in which one or other of the parties to an intergroup situation insists upon regarding the other group as different and pursues policies other than 'pluralistic' ones towards it.

We may take it that minority problems do not concern us, when a minority group seeks assimilation and is granted the right to assimilate, or, when it seeks pluralistic coexistence and is accorded the right to and even legal protection of this right of coexistence. Where this degree of agreement holds there would certainly be no race relations problem. This is what is meant when it is said that there is no such thing as 'good race relations'. What we should be concerned with are the situations in which conflict of aims exist and certain specific social processes are engendered as the parties pursue their conflict with one another.

The most common situation in which poor immigrant minorities find themselves is that in which they wish to be assimilated, but are denied the right to do so by their hosts. In this case a number of possibilities open up. The obvious one is the assignment of the minority to inferior rôles only, that is to say their segregation, particuarly with regard to where they live and the occupations they are allowed to follow. This apparently is what Simpson and Yinger mean by 'continued subjugation'. Whether or not this alternative is followed, however, depends upon how far the members of dominant groups require the services of the minority.

If it were the case that the minority's services were unnecessary, the 'host' view might well be that it would be best if they disappeared from the scene either through their enforced departure to other countries or, more radically, through their extermination. In fact it might be difficult to find an instance in which a group seeking assimilation was simply exterminated by a host society which opposed its assimilation. In the case of the Jews, for example, there were the additional circumstances that the minority did not seek complete assimilation, and that it was also a convenient scapegoat.

So far as enforced population transfer is concerned, this certainly is something which is often discussed by host society representatives, both in the case of groups which wish to assimilate, and in the case of those which wish to maintain their separate identity. Where such discussion takes place, however, it may have two possible meanings. It may be put forward as a genuine policy proposal, or it may be put forward as a means of increasing hostility towards the group and reinforcing the case against its being assimilated. In either case, however, one would have a case in which it was being urged that membership of a group was *prima facie* evidence for the assignment of an individual to a position of relative rightlessness in the society. It should be noted that a group could be subject to this kind of propaganda, even though it was not discriminated against in the narrow sense. Thus a common policy view in Britain in the nineteen-sixties was that which said that although those coloured immigrants who had established themselves were entitled to equal rights no more of their kind should be admitted, and as many as possible should be persuaded or forced to leave.

Where minorities seek pluralistic coexistence, secession or the right to emigrate and are opposed in their wishes, one might also face the fact of ascriptive rôle allocation at least by the group which wishes to maintain its separate existence and hence the makings of a racial problem. The problem here from a sociological point of view is not, of course, which group is to blame, or which group pursues 'racialist' policies. The sociological problem is simply that there is a conflict of aims regarding whether or not a group shall have a separate existence or not. In such circumstances a number of outcomes are possible. Where pluralistic integration is sought and denied the 'host' group might either 'persecute' the minority for trying to practise its traditional way of life, may seek to expel it from the country, or may even think of exterminating it, while the minority concerned would be forced into a kind of clandestine existence. Where a group seeks secession without migration and is denied it, the powerful host group may enforce tighter and tighter central government control while the minority might resort to revolutionary tactics ranging from passive resistance through sabotage to terrorism and military rebellion.

Turning from simple situations concerning immigrant minorities to some of those which we mentioned earlier, we should now consider a different case, namely that in which two or more find themselves competing for resources. In this case we have something more like the classic situation of conflict theory. The parties are engaged in a zero-sum game. The more one gets the less is available to the other. In this case, the expectation is that each group will do all that it can to restrict the right to compete of the other. The structure of the problem here is similar, whether we are dealing with a metropolitan or a colonial country, and whatever the arena of competitition. In any case the same formal possibilities exist. One party will seek the extermination of the other, its enforced departure from the country or its confinement to inferior positions. Thus nomadic settlers competing for land with indigenous colonial people have sometimes simply exterminated them. In post-colonial situations trading minorities have been expelled to make way for indigenous business men, and 'job reservation' for particular ethnic groups is a common tactic in countries like South Africa, where different groups compete to control particular kinds of employment.

A new dimension is added to any of the situations mentioned if a minority group which has been identified comes to be regarded as a scapegoat. In this case the dynamics of intergroup relations will be determined, not merely by the conflict situation, but by the fact that there is internal conflict and strain within the social structure and within the value system. What must follow in these circumstances is the pursuit of a policy towards the minority which is not quite covered by any of the alternatives which Simpson and Yinger mention. Extermination of the minority is, of course, a useful policy, but only so long as it lasts. Clearly, if such a policy were pursued far enough it would lead to the killing of the goose that laid the golden egg of what Parsons would call 'pattern maintenance and tension management'.[4] Nor, on the other hand, would continued subjugation be sufficient in itself. It is not merely that the group should be deprived. That could occur without it being made clear that tension and anger on the part of the ruling group should be directed against the minority. For this rituals of one kind or another have to be devised. If possible the members of the minority must be brought before the courts for offences not merely against the law, but against what is thought of as common morality, they must be found guilty and given exemplary sentences. And it will be important not merely that the courts act in this way, but that all 'influentials' in the ruling group press home the lesson through their sermons, their newspaper articles and any other means of persuasion available.

In so far as the dynamic of such procedure lies in the stresses and strains of the host societies' structure and value system, one

4. Parsons, Shils, *et. al.*, *Theories of Society, loc. cit.*

might be inclined to say that, if these stresses and strains abated, so also would the intensity of the punitive policies directed against minorities. For instance, in so far as the minority was being blamed for circumstances of economic crisis, an improvement of economic circumstances would lead to an abatement of scapegoating. This may in part be true, but there also seems to be some evidence that once a group is identified in this way, a particular view of the group and the treatment to which it is entitled might become built into the culture. In that case one would expect the intensity of the punishments to be magnified with each new upswing of the crisis. Some such process might have been involved in the development of European antisemitism. In that case only military defeat of the society in which it had become so central a feature finally put a stop to the process of continuous intensification.

The fourth alternative which we mentioned above was the case in which one group systematically exploits the labour of the other. This is quite a different case from any of those mentioned above and it is, of course, the paradigmatic colonial case. Here, after conquest, the exploited group are put to work and an elaborate system of sanctions and a supporting ideology are developed in order to maintain them in an inferior position. Extermination is not, of course, a sensible policy, since it is not possible to exploit those whom one has exterminated. It has, of course, sometimes been an accidental by-product of too intensive exploitation, as for example in the Spanish settlers dealings with American Indians in some territories, but it was not a deliberate policy. Again there is no point whatever in deportation. It may be discussed as a part of the general attempt to vilify the exploited group and thereby make them exploitable, but that is another matter. The main point is the systematic development of its controls by the group in power. Of course the more such controls are built up the more the exploited group are liable to move towards revolution particularly if they can obtain outside aid. But it is significant that revolutionary change in such a society does need outside aid. So long as the ruling group itself remains undivided it is usually quite capable of exercising enough control to keep any purely internal revolution from getting off the ground.

These considerations are well illustrated by the postwar history of the Union of South Africa. Despite increasing sophistication, education, industrial skills and ability to take collective action amongst the African population since 1945, the ruling white groups have (a) become more united in their resistance to the demands of the Africans and (b) ever more severe in the forms of control they have exercised. They have even sought to prevent incipient revolution by educating the African to believe in his own inferiority. Similar developments, of course, occurred in the case of the North American colonies which practised slavery. In both cases the system of white supremacy which was established proved virtually unshakeable by internal resistance. In the South African case, African hopes of change have come to depend upon military revolt led by invading guerrillas. It might also depend upon other outside agencies, such as new forms of business enterprise. So far, however, these have found it convenient to accept the forms of control which the government has established.

The final case which we noted in which one group acts towards the members of the other as a group, is that in which the various segments within the society are virtually at war with one another, and in which the nearest thing to social order is that which is achieved in the truce between intercommunal riots. To speak of one group discriminating against another in these circumstances would be an absurd understatement. What is at issue is the question of who controls the society. So long as a third party more powerful than either group controlled the society politically by keeping all groups without political rights they could coexist. But in the post-colonial situation one group usually takes command and if it is challenged may very well respond by demanding the expulsion of the challengers or by licensing their extermination in intercommunal rioting.

Some would seek the causes of such intercommunal troubles

in ex-colonial territories as explicable in terms of the economic rôles of the various groups. If that were so it might be possible to assimilate this case to the one mentioned previously. But it is precisely because the absolute right to the legitimate use of violence is not controlled by any one group that this inter-communal case has the features which it does. It could well be that in a period in which the technologically advanced nations had withdrawn from the business of colonialism cases of this kind might be the most common form of what would in all likelihood be called racialism.

Obviously, from all that has been said, we cannot accept the usage which makes 'racialism' the practice of discrimination by one group against another because of its physical character-istics. Colour discrimination itself includes a variety of different situations for the coloured group and a wide variety of policies pursued towards the group. As we have seen it might mean denial of admission to the full social, political and legal rights of citizenship in an advanced country; it might mean unfair com-petition against a coloured group with regard to some facility; it might mean that the group is made a scapegoat; it might mean that it is assigned to a position of rightlessness and economically exploited; and it might mean that the group faces hostility in an inter-communal situation. 'Discrimination', moreover, might turn out to mean that the group is forced either to assimilate or to be segregated; it might be held in an inferior position in the society; it might seek secession and be forcibly denied the right to secede; it might be denied the right to emigrate; it might be forced to emigrate to another country or to a segregated area of the same country; it might be subject to punitive policies and it might be destined for extermination.

But this same wide range of hostile policies in intergroup situations may be pursued against groups which are not recog-nisable by some physical characteristic. True, physical features like colour can operate as very effective criteria for distinguish-ing a group and they are more irradicable than cultural charac-teristics like the practice of Jewish or Roman Catholic religion.

But the important distinction is not between physical and cultural characteristics as criteria, so much as how these criteria are regarded. It seems clear that there are situations and societies in which the rôles to which people are assigned and the rights to which they are thought to be entitled, are dependent upon their achievement in some sphere in which variable achievement is possible. On the other hand, there are societies in which rôles and rights are assigned on the basis of possession or non-possession of some characteristic thought to be of a fixed kind. Whether this is a physical or a cultural characteristic is not of itself important.

It does not appear to us to be necessary to use the term racialism to refer to the various types of hostile policy pursued towards these groups. All that we are saying at this point is that it is a feature of some social systems and social situations that individuals are assigned to positions on the basis of ascriptive criteria, and that some of the groups thus formed become the target or focus for hostile policies of one sort or another. This gives us a narrower range of situations than we discussed in Chapters Two, Three and Four, but a wider range than those in which specific types of theoretical justification are offered for hostile intergroup policies.

It will clarify our position still further if we consider for a moment the way in which the term racialist is most commonly used. It has usually been used to refer to hostile policies directed against coloured people and Jews. When attempts have been made to systematise and rationalise this usage, however, the meaning attached to the term has changed in two directions. In the case of 'discrimination' against coloured people the term racialism was explained as referring to the *practice* of discrimination on the basis of relatively objectively observable characteristics. In the case of anti-semitism, however, there were no such clear physical characteristics, and this kind of racialism was therefore defined as the practice which followed from a false *theory*. Thereafter, the simplest way of sorting out the confusion was to say that racism was the appropriate term to use when discussing theories and racialism when discussing practice.

As we have said, this is a confusing oversimplification. In our view, there are three relatively distinguishable aspects of what we call race relations situations. Firstly there are certain distinctive structural features of the social situation concerned having to do with the kind of stratification and the degree of pluralism. In those cases which concern us there is always a high potentiality for conflict inherent in the situation. Amongst these situations, however, there are some in which groups rather than individuals are parties to the conflict. That is to say, groups do not form, as Marx's classes in themselves were assumed to form, *in the course* of the conflict. Their existence is recognised as *preceding* the conflict so that conflict positions are assigned in terms of recognisable group characteristics. Whether or not the conduct of one group towards another in situations which are structured in this way is called racialist it is obviously extremely important sociologically speaking. But thirdly and finally, within this class of situations we distinguish a narrower sub-class according to the principles or theory in terms of which discrimination between one group and another is justified.

Yet this is to oversimplify. The three stages to which we refer are only *relatively* distinguishable from one another. In particular the distinction which we have made between theory and practice cannot be absolutely sustained. As soon as we seek to analyse social interaction or a pattern of social relations in terms of the action frame of reference, we are forced to recognise that the model of social interaction which we use in our analysis posits a cognitive element in the form of the 'typifications' in terms of which participant actors are thought of as preparing themselves for action. What we do very often is to seek to understand action in terms of the principles, including cognitive or intellectual ones, which underly it. We do not thereby imply that men consciously think out their courses of action on an abstract theoretical level, but we do make it impossible to distinguish absolutely between thought and action and theory and practice.

Just as the distinction between our second and third levels of analysis is difficult to maintain in an absolute form, so also is that between the first and the second. There are no pure structures which assume the operation of no intellectual or cognitive principles any more than there are theories unrelated to implicit principles of action. What we are really dealing with is a unitary phenomenon whose operation is seen most clearly on the second level of analysis. There we see theory and structure related to one another, and this is hence the most important level of all. But there are occasions on which it is useful to emphasise the structure or the theory depending upon the purpose of our enquiry. We may, for instance, wish to locate the structural source of the conflict which expresses itself in intergroup hostility, or we may be concerned with the integration of a society's belief system or value system.

In laying the emphasis on the second level of analysis, however, we are making a point of some strategic importance for race relations studies. There are those who see the study of race relations as reducible to purely structural problems, particularly those concerned with stratification, and there are those who confine it to situations in which racist theories are in evidence. In our view, whatever terminology we use, the analysis of intergroup conflict of the kinds we have described in this chapter is a topic of central sociological importance which cannot be completely absorbed into stratification theory, the theory of the plural society, the sociology of knowledge or the history of ideas.

We will show in the next chapter that the systematisation of the principles of intergroup action at the level of belief systems and value systems is of some independent causal significance, and it might well be argued that it is only those situations which have distinguishable features on this level which properly fall within the field of the study of race relations. This may be, but it is none the less true that the pay-off of any independent developments at the level of belief and value systems is to be found at the level of intergroup action. Moreover, it is quite possible that once a set of beliefs is effectively built into the system of social interaction, the need for its explicit formulation and annunciation is less evident, in which case the theory will only be found in the practice.

Most important of all, we should notice the problems posed for us by the political and ideological context of race relations studies in the latter part of the twentieth century. We live in a period in which the systematic theoretical justifications of inter-group hostility which were so prominent in the nineteen thirties have been nearly universally discredited, at least so far as official policy statements are concerned. But this does not by any means imply that the theory has not been built into the practice, and that the same policies are pursued against the same groups as those which used to be called racist. Thus for example, one would not expect leaders of the main political parties in Western Europe publicly to support racist theory. One may find none-theless that they pursue the same policies towards minority groups but find different justifications and rationalisations for them. Where this is the case, a simple assertion that racialism no longer exists is either politically and sociologically naïve or has the effect of restricting race relations studies to a politically insignificant area.

We would argue that the study of hostile policies directed towards groups ascriptively distinguished by either physical or cultural characteristics should be a central area of study for sociologists, and that the study of race relations must find its subject matter somewhere within this field. On the one hand there will be some situations in which the hostile policies are explicitly justified and rationalised in terms of racist theory, and these are obviously to be included as core race relations studies. On the other there are cases in which racist assumptions are implicit in the policies pursued and in which it is the task of the sociologist of race relations to understand them.

The further narrowing down of the field through the definition of what kinds of theories are racist is the topic of our next chapter. As we shall see, this is itself no easy problem, but we should not allow this to prevent us from recognising the common properties of the larger class of situations which we have been discussing.

6. Racism

When the World War of 1939–1945 came to an end, the United Nations and its various agencies made a systematic attempt to deal with what were regarded as being the roots of racism and racialism, or more specifically, the roots of problems like anti-semitic theories and practice in Nazi Germany. The easiest way in which these problems could be dealt with was by referring them to committees of intellectuals who concerned themselves with that aspect of the problem with which they, by their training, were best fitted to deal. The result has been that a great deal of the analytic work which has been done on the problems of race relations at this level has overemphasised the importance of the relatively systematic theories in terms of which hostile policies towards particular groups were justified.

To put such studies in perspective it might perhaps be useful to recall some of the basic analytic concepts used by Pareto[1] in his analysis of social action. According to Pareto the theories which men offered as explaining their actions had to be taken as secondary manifestations of the same sentiments as led to the action to be explained. If one looked at these theories one would find that despite the tremendous variety of justifications of action which were offered there were certain constant 'residues' in all of them. The residues were the basic non-logical theories which would help us to understand what men were really about. Since, however, men were rationalising creatures they liked to give some kind of intellectual justification to their actions and so bolstered their basic non-logical reasons for acting with false

1. V. Pareto, *Mind and Society*, Harcourt, Brace and Company, New York, 1935.

arguments, appeals to authority and so on. These latter justifications Pareto called 'derivations'.

We do not agree wholly with Pareto's analysis. In particular, it seems misleading to suggest that the residues are simply the causal product of sentiments. As we see it, men act and interact in accordance with their interests or in conformity with norms which they accept for one reason or another. We cannot accept that there are basic psychological types of irrational behaviour at the root of all conduct. On the other hand we do accept, with Pareto, that the reasons which men give in order to account systematically for their behaviour are added after the behaviour is complete, and are not adequate to account for it. This means that we think it to be an important part of the analysis of social structures and interaction that we should explore the full variety of derivations which occur, when one group pursues hostile policies against another. If we do this, we shall avoid the misleading notion that these policies are the product of false theories and that if the theories are challenged the policies will cease.

An alternative approach to that which emphasises systematic racist theories is that which emphasises the study of attitudes. This is the approach of empiricist psychology to the study of race relations. It assumes that there are measurable tendencies to action by individuals, that one can find out to what extent particular tendencies exist in a population and what factors are correlated with the presence or absence of these tendencies.

Such an approach is a valuable corrective to that which over-emphasises highly articulate and systematic theory. It does emphasise action elements mobilised at the point of action. It is defective, however, in not seeking to understand and explain the tendencies to action called attitudes and hence represents them as static 'things'. What we wish to consider is the relationship between these mental elements, social action and interaction, and the social structure.

Our focus is on understanding society rather than personality, or to put the matter another way, our concept of personality is a sociological one. As Simpson and Yinger put it,

From our point of view personality is best conceived not as a collection of traits, not as a static system . . . but as a process . . . the process of carrying out functions of a shop steward in a union, superintendent of schools, or 'courteous customer' does not allow full individual variation to come into play. The rôles themselves have some compulsions that influence which of the various tendencies which the individual will express.[2]

We might perhaps express a slight doubt about the use of the term 'rôle' in this context, in that the term does sometimes seem to refer to total and integrated social systems, whereas what we have in mind includes a variety of different types of socially governed action, ranging from the mobilisation of actors for collective action in order to achieve their interests to action which is completely governed by norms and rules. With this reservation, however, we can certainly accept Simpson and Yinger's formulation. The important point is that we are concerned, not merely with individual personality systems, but with the effect on individual conduct of social structures and social situations.

Our approach to the study of racist theory also has much in common with recent approaches to the sociology of knowledge, most notably that of Berger and Luckmann in their *Social Construction of Reality*.[3] If, in general, their approach over-emphasises the cognitive element in social interaction, so far as our present concern goes this is not relevant, for we are especially concerned here with the way in which ideas influence and are involved in interaction. At the same time Berger and Luckmann's book has the very great merit of recognising that 'knowledge' influences action not merely at highly abstract theoretical levels but in humble and humdrum ways at the level of social interaction in everyday life. This Schutzian perspective[4]

2. G. E. Simpson and J. M. Yinger, 'Sociology of Race and Ethnic Relations' in Merton, Broom and Cottrell, *Sociology Today*, Basic Books, New York, 1959, p. 379.

3. B. L. Berger and T. Luckmann, *The Social Construction of Reality*, Allen Lang, London, 1967.

4. A. Schutz, *Collected Papers*, Vol. I, *The Problem of Social Reality*, Martinus Nijhoff, The Hague, 1967.

is especially important for us, in that we are concerned in the study of racism precisely with the rôle of ideas in everyday life. The renewed emphasis on the sociology of knowledge as the precondition of all sociology, and of a cognitive element as the precondition of action, has occurred because writers in the phenomenological and symbolic interactionist traditions have recognised that it is only possible for one actor to 'orient his conduct to another' if it is possible for these two actors to share the same intersubjective world. Thus, long before actors in specialised rôles can sit down and reason and argue about the world in abstract terms, other actors at the grass roots must have agreed to attribute common meanings to their experience. There is a sense, indeed, in which we must all 'prejudge' our experience, because, if we were not able to catch the fleeting moments of that experience in terms of 'typifications', 'ideal types' or stereotypes, we would not be able to share that experience with anybody else.

We create an intersubjective world of physical objects by agreeing to attach labels to our experience. In doing this, we make the claim that they are in some sense the same experiences that other people have had, and we also connect them with other experiences of our own, in that meanings do not stand by themselves but have definite relations to each other. Thus when I say that I see a cat, I am saying that I am having an experience which is similar to some of your experiences, and which has clear relationships of similarity and dissimilarity to other experiences, such as that which I describe as seeing a dog. In using language about the physical world, therefore, human beings must already be assumed to hold implicit shared theories about the world and how it works.

Such a mapping of the world and what is in it by a group of actors is not, however, simply a cognitive business. For at this level of 'theorising' no distinction is made between merely claiming that something exists and giving instructions as to how it should be treated, or saying whether it is good, beautiful or sacred. Thus one assumes that the process of teaching, whereby an Arunta boy in Central Australia was taught that a certain object was a 'churinga', was the starting point for a whole process of scientific, aesthetic, moral and religious education. He could really only learn what a 'churinga' was in a complete sense by understanding the whole set of concepts implicit in the totemic culture.[5]

Our culture is, of course, distinguished by the fact that, so far as the objects of the physical world are concerned, we do try to distinguish the question, 'what is this object?', from all questions about its aesthetic and other qualities. Thus there is a set of agreed procedures called 'science' by which we arrive at a picture of the world which is held to be most relevant for a number of purposes. But, even in our culture, this is not always the most relevant picture. There is little point, for instance, in a scientific demonstration of the chemical properties of the substances used in religious sacraments, any more than there is in a geometric analysis and a description of a painting. For these purposes other procedures for reaching agreement than those of natural science are resorted to.

In everyday life, however, distinctions of this kind are not made and the structuring of interaction in a social way depends upon their not being made. There is no society, not even our own, with its highly scientistic culture, in which the teaching of language is not used to impose an initial normative order upon the pupil, long before he learns explicit moral rules. This is quite obvious in the case of the opportunistic way in which we impose taboos on our children by drumming into them that, say, eating coal is nasty. But it goes far beyond this. What we imagine is a purely factual world is shot through with moral meanings.

But, if this is true in the case of the shared intersubjective world of physical objects which our language creates for us, how much more is it true of the world of social objects. Here 'scientific' techniques for discriminating between the question

5. C. E. Durkheim, *The Elementary Forms of Religious Life*, Allen and Unwin, London, 1954, Book 2.

'what is this?' and the question 'how should I feel or act towards this?' are ill developed and, even if they were fully developed, it is unlikely that they would influence everyday action to anything like the same extent that the scientific picture of the physical world does. The goal of positivism from Comte to Lundberg[6] has, of course, always been that this should be the case, and that not merely sociologists but the man in the street should think scientifically about the social world; but it is a goal which has clearly not been realised.

It is not clear, in any case, what exactly a 'scientific' way of looking at and labelling social objects or other human beings would be. Even the assertion 'this is a human being', set against the assertion 'this is a Jew' or 'this is a negro', may involve implicit reference to some moral or political code, which asserts that the differences between men are less important than their similarities, and that being human as such imposes certain moral claims. Thus we should not be surprised to find that there is no known society in which social actors are not categorised in terms much narrower than 'human being'.

The simplest form of categorisation is that which is given in a system of kinship terminology. This means any participant actor in a primitive society is able to attach to any other participant, not merely a personal name, but a position term, so that it is clear what rights and duties the other participant has, not merely *vis-à-vis ego*, but *vis-à-vis* every other individual. Within a system of this kind we may say that rights and rôles are particularistically and ascriptively defined. They take the form 'X is your grandfather and therefore he has certain rights and duties in relation to you. Necessarily he must have certain other rights and duties to each category of your relatives.' There will, however, also be certain groups whose relationship to *ego* cannot be defined in terms of kinship terminology. Some of these will be grouped in classificatory groups such as clans, and the position of an individual *vis-à-vis* an individual in another group will follow from the relationship which any individual in the one

6. G. Lundberg, *Foundations of Sociology*, Macmillan, New York, 1939.

group is held to have with any member of the other. In this case rights and rôles may be said to be defined in an ascriptive but classificatory way.

To say this is, of course, by no means to say that such an intergroup relationship has any of the elements which we noted as typifying a race relations situation. A social system based upon normative consensus, and involving no elements of conflict or coercion, may be built up in this way. Indeed it seems to be a very common kind of system in primitive tribes particularly those with clan totems. What differentiates such a system from that which we shall presently be discussing in composite societies, is that the classificatory and ascriptive allocation of rights and duties is a means of achieving a division of labour, through which overall group ends, as well as the ends of the various parties, can be attained. There is no question of the group which is singled out in this way becoming the target of hostile policies. Such may be the case so far as people who fall right outside of the tribe or its constituent clans are concerned, and at this point there may be parallels with race relations problems (as for example in the case of neighbouring tribes with a long tradition of emnity like the Kikuyu and the Masai in Kenya). But even with regard to outsiders to the tribe, the image of the other may be more negative than positive. He is an individual, who is beyond the range within which it is possible to define rights and duties, rather than simply as an enemy.

It should, perhaps, be noted that we have made a distinction so far between rôles and rights being defined on an ascriptive and *particularistic* basis on the one hand, and an ascriptive and *classificatory* basis on the other. We thus revert to using the term which Morgan used in his discussion of kinship terminology, rather than the term 'universalism' which Parsons contrasts with particularism.[7] We do so because, while we believe that it is worth while making a distinction between situations in which individuals are treated as members of groups and categories and situations in which they are treated as individuals,

7. L. Morgan, *Ancient Society*, Henry Holt, New York, 1877.

yet we think that the term 'universalism' is misleading. It may be that it has simply been linked so much with the concept of 'achievement-orientation' by Parsons, that some of the meaning of that concept has rubbed off on to universalism, but the term itself seems to suggest a society which is meritocratic and based upon the rule of law with no place for nepotism. For the limited type of non-particularism which we have in mind, therefore, the simple term classificatory seems more appropriate.

On the other hand, of course, we do not use this term in Morgan's sense. He was concerned to compare the systems of kinship terminology of the advanced societies having isolated conjugal families with those of primitive societies where kinship was the rule. But we are concerned with the contrast between one total system and another. From this point of view, all kinship systems are, relatively speaking, particularistic, and it seems that, beyond the particularistic categories of kinship terminologies, primitive people are bound to resort to classificatory categories of one kind or another. Examples of verbalised responses of this kind are frequent in the literature of race relations. In our second chapter we quoted the Spanish historian who referred to the American Indians as a naturally 'lazy and vicious, melancholic, cowardly and in general a lying shiftless people'.[8] Similarly the first Governor of the Cape Colony referred to the Hottentots as 'stupid, dull, stinking people'.[9] And one could quote statements like this from many colonial, immigrant and, indeed, class situations.

It could be argued that statements like these are the result of false beliefs of a more generalised kind and we would admit that such reactions do not result simply from immediate perceptions and experience. None the less it is important to recognise that, if there is any 'theoretical' element in such statements, it is of an elementary and implicit kind. A situation where the typifications which one group has of another are of this direct kind, is far removed from that in which the perception of the member of the

8. L. Hanke, *loc. cit.*
9. C. W. de Kiewet, *A History of South Africa*, Oxford, 1946, p. 20.

other group is conditioned by widely believed pre-existing theories.

What we are saying then is that in relatively complex social systems individuals react to each other in classificatory and ascriptive ways, and that sometimes the other who is reacted to in this way is also the target for hostile attitudes and policies. This, of course, is particularly likely to be the case in situations, such as those discussed in our first four chapters, in which distinguishable groups find themselves in situations of conflict or competition with one another. The basic and, in one sense, the objective facts of the situation are that the two groups find themselves in a state of competition with one another. But subjectively this state of competition results in attitudes of emnity and the verbalisations to which they give rise. Instead of the somewhat intellectualised response 'this type of person is my competitor and in attempting to realise my goals I have to stop him attaining his' one finds the much simpler response 'these people are evil'. It is arguable that statements of this kind, and certainly the attitudes which underlie them before they are verbalised, are as much forms of aggression resulting from frustration in the objective situation as they are deductions from theory.

It is also worth noting here that, as racist theories have become more disreputable, ways have been found of giving *intellectualised* expression to attitudes of hostility which make little appeal to complex theories at all. Thus one finds in contemporary Britain that a commonly expressed attitude to coloured people is simply this: 'We have nothing against you. You may be as good as us. But we don't want you here. And since we, like you, have a right to our own separate existence there is nothing wrong or racialist or immoral about our saying this.' Thus a way is found of expressing intergroup hostility, which has nothing of the intellectual disreputableness of racist theory, and also avoids immediate emotive sounding statements of hostility.

This kind of intergroup hostility to which we are referring may, it is true, be found, wherever there is an element of competition in the relation between groups. Orwell has noted that he and his fellow public schoolboys in England in the thirties all believed that the working classes stank,[10] and no doubt similar reactions could be discovered in other ethnically homogeneous societies. Such reactions do not contradict our thesis, for we have not said that they were confined to interracial situations. They are, however, far more likely when the groups concerned appear to each other as alien and foreign.

A particularly interesting recent phenomenon has been seen in the development, in the American negro revolution, of assertions which are the direct opposite of those common amongst the ruling white group. Thus, whereas throughout the history of American society the whites have not merely made their own assertions about the negro's negative qualities, but have even required that the negro himself believed them, today politically articulate negroes are deliberately attempting to instil into negro children positive evaluations of their own qualities and negative evaluations of the whites. Thus the children are taught that 'black is beautiful' and that all white people are 'pigs'. Many liberal whites are appalled by these assertions and express their regret at negro 'racialism', but they are the exact equivalent of the expressions of sentiment which have been taken for granted for centuries in white dominated society.

Before we continue by considering the way in which these elementary expressions of one group's reaction to another are rationalised and developed into more articulate systems of thought, we might profitably consider the theoretical structure of what we ourselves are saying, and its relation to certain classical positions in sociological theory. In particular we should note the relationship between what we are saying and Marx's conception of the economic base and ideological superstructure on the one hand and Pareto's conception of residues and sentiments on the other.

We saw earlier the importance of Pareto's notion of 'derivations' as the attempt which men make to rationalise their

10. G. Orwell, *The Road to Wigan Pier*, Left Book Club, London, 1939.

actions after the event and the contrast which had to be made between these derivations and the 'constant part' (the residues) which explained their action. We should now note the point which Parsons made so forcibly in his analysis of Pareto's thought,[11] *viz.* that the residues are not simply sentiments or instincts, but essentially non-logical theories of action. Similarly we are trying here to distinguish between attempts to justify and rationalise action on a fairly high theoretical level and the simple and elementary evaluations which one group makes of another, but would not by any means wish to claim that these were in any sense primary instinctive reactions. What we are talking about are elementary verbal guides to action as contrasted with complex theories.

We do wish to assert, however, that such elementary reactions are not simply deductions from explicit theories on a higher level (though they may be strengthened by their relationship to such theories). We would therefore argue that they are in part caused by men's reactions to their enemies and competitors in some kind of basic struggle to survive or earn a living. Clearly Marx was right in insisting that, at this level, one was not dealing with some kind of psychological cause, as are other sociologists such as Oppenheimer, who see the business of conquest rather than economic exploitation as the basic process. But both economic competition and exploitation on the one hand, and military struggle on the other, do produce psychological reactions of aggression, and these reactions are verbalised in the form of elementary statements and stereotypes which we have been discussing. Thus both Pareto and the Marxists are emphasising part of the truth. What we have in intergroup relations is a succession of the following elements: (*a*) a process of conflict, competition or struggle for survival between groups, (*b*) psychological reactions of aggression and hostility on the part of members of one group against members of the other, (*c*) verbal expressions of this hostility asserting that the other group

11. T. Parsons, *The Structure of Social Action*, Free Press, Glencoe, 1949, Chapter 5.

has undesirable qualities or demanding that in some way it should cease to exist. Beyond this there are a number of further stages which would seem to belong to the area of what Marxists call the superstructure and Pareto 'derivations'. What we wish to insist on is that, despite the verbalisations involved at this level, it has to be distinguished from the more explicit theorising level.

In order to understand this other level and the way in which it operates, we must now set out the kind of intellectual and theoretical problem to which the pursuit of hostile intergroup policies with the accompanying verbalisations is likely to give rise. We assume that human beings will always give reasons for their actions if they can, and that the problem now is to explain why a group of people, recognisable through their possession of some physical or cultural characteristic, should have the further attributes which leads to their being subject to negative evaluations and hostile policies. The answer to this might simply take the form of the cataloguing of further alleged facts about the group's characteristics and behaviour in an *ad hoc* empirical manner, or may involve some overall theoretical explanation which starts by spelling out the essential qualities of the group in question and seeks to show that observed behaviour or behaviour alleged to have been observed follows from these essential characteristics.

Everyone who has participated in the debate about the rights of coloured people, Jews or other minority groups knows that commonly the debate amongst non-sociological laymen and amongst practical politicians takes the form of an argument about what the facts of the case are. But the experienced debater of these issues will also be aware that any final demonstration of and agreement about what facts exist is impossible. The argument twists and turns, and, whenever one of the contenders is apparently pinned down on one logical level, he quickly changes his ground so that the issue is taken up on a new level. This may best be illustrated by examples.

The campaign to secure a cessation of coloured immigration into Britain, and, indeed, the repatriation of established immigrants, is supported by what claim to be factual assertions about individual cases and by statistical generalisations. But immediately these assertions are challenged new questions open up about how such facts are to be evaluated anyway.

Thus a well-known Conservative politician, who has for some time been advocating the cessation of coloured immigration, adduces in support of his policy proposals 'evidence' to the effect that he has been told that there is a street in his constituency where there is only one white person left, and that she, an old lady, has been terrorised by immigrants, who amongst other things have put their excreta through her letter box. Investigations by journalists show that there is only one old lady who lives in anything like the situation described, that she likes and is liked by her immigrant neighbours, that she has not had excreta put through her letter box and that she is distressed that the politician concerned might have created hostility between herself and her neighbours.

As this argument proceeds the Conservative politician and his supporters question whether the old lady interviewed by the journalists is the one in question, and argue that whether or not the original old lady exists in the conditions described, the fact that people believe she does is the important thing. Hence, if interracial hostility is not to increase, it would be best if coloured immigrants did not exist. So the argument changes its ground, and will change it again, as soon as it appears to be finally pinned down to a purely factual question.

Again the issue of the presence of large numbers of coloured children in certain schools might be represented as a threat to the education of the native white children and the reason given for this is that coloured children are unable to speak the language in which instruction is normally given. When it is pointed out that West Indian coloured children speak English, whereas many Cypriot or Italian children do not, either we are told that West Indian children do not speak English properly, or the ground of the argument shifts, and we are told 'it isn't only a question of language'.

On the level of statistics the grounds for manoeuvre in the argument are even easier to come by. Thus, if it is argued that statistics show that the number of immigrants is less than is widely supposed, arguments might be produced to show that there are possibilities of illegal entry, or that births to the immigrants are not adequately and separately recorded. The number of coloured immigrant mothers occupying maternity beds is quoted as compelling evidence which is not easily shaken by estimates of what would happen if coloured immigration ceased and the coloured immigrants' places were taken by others. The argument more generally about the charge represented by the immigrants on the social services readily passes to an argument about whether or not it is right that every penny spent on immigrants should be treated as a dead loss. And so it seems every argument about statistics is likely to develop. We are not of course, concerned with the question of how the problem might be resolved by competent statisticians (though they too will usually be found to be capable of finding reasons for disagreement amongst themselves). The important thing is which arguments can be made to hold water in the actual practical and political conditions in which the debate is conducted. Here it would seem the argument can be made to go on *ad infinitem*, and the mere continuance of the argument serves to mark out the group whose rights are being discussed and to bring those rights into question. Thus, if anyone wished as a matter of deliberate policy to increase hostility towards a group a possible guiding rule might be 'Get the argument going by whatever assertions you can muster. Once it is going you will find that the facts don't speak for themselves. With skill you can make them speak for you.'

It should not be imagined from what we have just said that conscious or unconscious distortion is the prerogative of the 'reactionary' side of this argument. In political debate the 'liberals' will also deploy their arguments and statistics in a way which leads to the conclusions which they want accepted. Even the man who tries to be as honest as possible finds it difficult to produce a finally compelling argument when any of his logical methodological, theoretical or factual assumptions might be called into question at any time. He is thus very often driven into a kind of dogmatism by the very conditions of the debate and once this has happened it can very readily be said that there is no way of deciding between alternative views.

It is obvious to the sociologist of knowledge or the sociologist of politics that what purport to be arguments about fact in this debate often conceal arguments about values. The reactionaries and the liberals have taken up their positions in advance and use facts selectively to support their positions. Moreover, as Myrdal has pointed out,[12] when there is some kind of strain between the society's ultimate value system and its actual behaviour towards certain ethnic minorities, there may be a positive compulsion to invent facts.

In the American situation Myrdal argued that a value system like the 'American creed' was so explicit that it was not possible to allow extensive racial discrimination without the support of some intervening beliefs which would justify the apparent departure from principles. Thus a general proposition in the American creed might take the form 'all men are entitled to equal opportunity in employment according to their ability'. The belief that negroes do not have equal intellectual ability with white people is therefore necessary to make the creed compatible with discriminatory practice.

Not every society, of course, has this problem in quite the acute form that American society does, for its ultimate value system has been set out in a Bill of Rights. None the less every society has its own myth, its own traditions and its own value system which requires some such intellectually reconciling process. In the case of Britain, for example, as in the case of ancient Rome, there has always existed some concept of British citizen-

12. G. Myrdal, *Value in Social Theory*, Routledge and Kegan Paul, London, 1958.

ship and the rights which pertained thereto. This was in part an ideological conception, it is true, which was designed to legitimise British domination of her colonies; but it none the less did have some importance, and if it did not lead to equal rights for all British citizens, it did at least require the elaboration of beliefs to bridge the gap between the ideal and the reality.

Ad hoc beliefs, however, are rarely sufficient to justify hostile behaviour towards a group. This may be the case to a greater extent in societies in which political empiricism and the belief in piecemeal social reform, as advocated by Popper,[13] is the rule. But there is amongst all men, and particularly in the more industrially advanced societies, some kind of drive towards consistency. Hence the particular sentiments, policies, evaluations and beliefs which we have been discussing will always find their place within some more overarching system of ideas. There need not necessarily be only one such system, and indeed there are often several competing systems available, but we must take account of these more general systems of ideas as one factor in any intergroup or any race relations situation.

There are two main dimensions in terms of which legitimating theories of this kind may be classified. On the one hand, we may classify them in terms of the degree to which they deal solely with the question 'what are the facts of the case?', separating this question from all problems of moral, aesthetic and other evaluation. The other is the extent to which the theory forms a closed logico-deductive system. Clearly the tendency of the most advanced natural sciences has been towards an extreme ideal type in which empirical questions are sharply distinguished from all others and in which the body of accepted propositions is regarded as in principle deducible from a few simple axioms. Only in the positivist's Utopia, however, could it be expected that the systematised beliefs which legitimate and sustain a social order could be of this kind.

At the other extreme from natural science in terms of the first

13. K. Popper, *The Poverty of Historicism*, Routledge and Kegan Paul, London, 1959.

of our dimensions is the set of ideas and practices which we call 'religion'. These are doubly non-empirical[14] in that they do not merely assert what the world is like but impose attitudes and behaviour on the believer and that they specifically refer to what Parsons calls non-empirical entities. In most societies, at most times in history, practices which arise in interpersonal relations and intergroup relations would become fully institutionalised and recognised in so far as they were shown to have some meaningful relation to the body of religious ideas and practice. In a society in which the logical type of reasoning to be found in science is highly prized, this meaningful relation will take on the form of a deductive system. Religion, that is to say, will have as one of its expressions, theology.

More generally 'culture' will have some of the aspects of religion. It, too, does not only refer to questions about what is the case, but imposes attitudes. In this case, however, the systematic interconnectedness would be one which depended upon relationships of meaning between symbols, rather than that which would be found in a logico-deductive system. Again, in every society, there will be pressure towards establishing a relationship of consistency between repeated forms of behaviour and the shared system of cultural meanings.

Falling somewhere between science and culture is the body of ideas which we refer to as history. By this we mean the body of ideas which is shared amongst the members of a population about its own and other people's past. It may be more or less systematic and it may segregate the question of what actually occurred, or what caused what, from other questions. It may, like science, concentrate on causal questions, or it may together with other cultural activities concentrate on exploring connections of symbolic meaning. In any case, however, 'history' will be one of the reference points in terms of which any people tries to make sense of and legitimate its day to day practices.

In complex societies, in which the social order is not accepted as an eternal one, all of the activities mentioned above are to

14. Parsons, *The Social System*, Chapter 8.

some extent changed as men come to accept Karl Marx's dictum that the task of 'philosophy' is not merely to interpret the world but to change it.[15] At this point, as Mannheim has so brilliantly shown,[16] the bodies of ideas and belief within a society become directed either towards changing or towards defending the *status quo*. The precise terminology which we should use to describe theoretical developments of this kind might be a matter of dispute. Marx would use the term 'ideology' to refer solely to the use of systematic thought by the ruling class to maintain its own rule. Mannheim uses the term in the same way, but links it with the term 'utopia' which refers to doctrines directed towards the promotion of change. Parsons and others have used the term ideology to cover both cases.[17] But whatever terminology is used, it is clear that doctrines such as these which are born out of the political struggle between progressives and conservatives are another reference point for the justification of intergroup relations.

The last contender for the rôle of intellectual and moral legitimator of social practice is social science, and particularly sociology. This term may be used to refer to a variety of forms of activity and intellectual doctrine, but running through all of them is some attempt to displace religious, cultural, historical and ideological affirmations with regard to social objects with others which approximate in form and character to those which are found in natural science. Obviously this takes an extreme form in the case of the positivist movement, which character-istically requires the formation of a positivist church. But it is in some degree the case with all sociology. Even the most moderate and explicitly anti-positivist sociologist would have to admit that in some degree he was submitting affirmations derived from these other fields to a new kind of analysis.

Science, religion, culture, history, ideology and sociology are

15. K. Marx, 'Theses on Feuerbach', in Marx and Engels, *Selected Works*, Vol. 2, p. 403.
16. K. Mannheim, *Ideology and Utopia*, Routledge and Kegan Paul, London.
17. Parsons, *The Social System*, Chapter 8.

terms which we use to describe the principal bodies of theoretical ideas which justify social practice in complex societies. In order to define them, we have referred to their more systematic forms. But we must now add, before going on to show how racialist practice is connected to these bodies of ideas, that any of them may be more or less systematic. Thoroughgoing systematisation of basic intellectual concepts has been a feature of only a few societies. Sometimes no complete systematisation has been carried through and sometimes a cultural preference has existed (as in the case of the empiricist bias of English thought) against systematisation. Moreover, even if a historical period is remembered by scholars because of the work of a great systematiser like Aquinas or Hegel, the fact is that only a small coterie of intellectuals shared the ideas of these great teachers. For the great majority of people life could be sustained and existing practices justified in terms of *ad hoc* maxims and proverbs rather than in terms of general and systematic theories.

In so-called mass societies, moreover, men obtain their ideas as to what the world, or some sector of it, is like, not from systematic, scientific or other theories, but from the foreshortened accounts of what has occurred, which are purveyed by the mass media. Thus, for example, a man in the English West Country town of Penzance, where few coloured people live, will learn, from the newspapers and from television programmes, that there are large numbers of coloured people in Wolverhampton, and that there is an argument going on about how this number should be limited. The man in Wolverhampton, who sees the same programme does not need to be told that there is a large number of coloured people in Wolverhampton, but the actual numbers and their likely increase are unknown to him, and for this information he might well be dependent upon the media. In *every* case the vast majority of the population will look to the media for guidance as to what the practical possibilities are of affecting their situation. Yet, so far as the question of coloured immigration in Britain is concerned, the media messages might well not include the information that the coloured immigrants are an essential part of the labour force, or that, as Commonwealth citizens, they have some special claim on the British economy. Whether or not people are aware of the nature of problems such as this, will depend very largely upon media messages and what they contain.

The content of the messages will, of course, be dependent upon the kinds of control of the mass media which operate in any particular society. In so far as a newspaper or a television programme is dependent for its income upon advertising in a mass market, information about the problems of intergroup relations will be conveyed in the course of entertainment of one kind or another, and the issues, whether they are actually falsified or not, are almost bound to be trivialised. On the other hand a growing minority of the population in advanced industrial countries obtains its information and its views from the so-called quality newspapers and journals, and from more serious radio and television programmes. It would be misleading to suggest that there was an absolute break between these quality journals and programmes, on the one hand, and the more popular media, on the other. What might, however, be noticed, is that there is a greater *tendency* towards systematisation in their handling of problems, and that they, far more than general scientific and historical theories, provide the intellectual justification and anchoring which supports the beliefs and attitudes which operate in everyday life.

Research in the area of mass communications has suggested that the media has less influence than is commonly supposed, because their messages are filtered in practice through local 'influentials', to whom most people look for guidance, before accepting what the mass media tell them. We would by no means wish to deny this finding, but its importance should not be misunderstood. The 'influentials' help those whom they influence to choose between the options available on the basis of information known to themselves. Thus, even if it were true that every message were filtered through them, it would still be the case that there was a message which originated entirely outside the local community.

In what is, in many ways, the most perceptive study of the effects on the structure of knowledge and society of mass communication, Richard Hoggart has shown that the values implicit in the messages of popular literature in Britain are based upon working class values, even though in their new form, they lack the moral tautness which they had in their original setting. It may be, in fact, that this linkage is the first of a series and that it should be the task of the sociology of knowledge to outline a kind of hierarchy of levels of beliefs and attitudes, information and theories, running from the values and beliefs of folk culture, through the world-views purveyed by the popular media and the foreshortened theories of the quality journals to the more systematic theories of science, religion, history and so on. Then, just as local influentials may be understood as channels and filters through whom information passes from the media to the folk community, so at other levels there will be liaison rôles for those who mediate between the world of serious journalism and the popular media and for those who popularise systematic scientific and other theories.

If such linkages exist it becomes a bit more meaningful to ask whether it makes a difference to a society if one scientific belief rather than another is held, for, while it may be the case that only a small number of individuals actually hold the belief, millions more might be influenced by it. Moreover, it is possible that the general characteristics of belief systems on the more abstract and systematic level might affect the whole structure of knowledge and belief in the society. It may then be possible to consider not merely whether a society is affected by racist theories of an abstract kind, but whether the characteristics of racism are in some way implicit in the whole structure of the society's thought.

We must now return to the question of the relevance of what we have been saying about belief systems and theories to problems of race relations. What need is it that these theories satisfy?

What intellectual difficulties are they used to overcome? To what extent are they a mere epiphenomenon and to what extent do they constitute causes of social activity?

The problem which 'discrimination' and the low level evaluative affirmations to which we referred earlier in this chapter pose for a society may be stated in a sharp and simplified form as follows: the individual finds himself saying 'These people are X's' and either pursuing hostile policies towards them, or claiming that they are 'stupid', that they are 'inferior', that they 'stink' and so on. An intellectual gap then has to be closed by showing why it is that people who are X's should have characteristics like being stupid or stinking, or characteristics which justify their receiving hostile treatment.

The one way of solving this problem which has been definitively singled out for discussion as racist is that which suggests that the connection concerned can be genetically established. That is to say, the evaluated quality attributed to the individual is treated as though it was a simple observable characteristic, and is said to depend upon the inherited chemical composition of the individual. The quality and the unequal entitlement to rights, which it seems to imply, are then said to be beyond human control.

Clearly this is an important case. If the assertion, which claims to be a scientific one were true, it would indeed make any programme of integration or of equalisation of rights much more difficult to justify. Not surprisingly, therefore, a great deal of intellectual effort has been devoted by liberals and humanists to its refutation. The problem which now faces us, however, in the light of its refutation is whether or not there are other doctrines which are functional equivalents. Let us consider some possible examples.

The most common perhaps is simply that which refers to stages of historical development amongst different peoples. Thus unequal treatment of a member of a particular group is commonly justified by saying 'This is not racial discrimination. It is simply a distinction which we make between men with differing degrees of education, culture, civilisation etc.' If it is then argued that particular individuals might perhaps skip historical stages, the reply would be that it would only be possible to obtain a superficial cultural veneer in that way. The actual acquisition of a culture or way of life, it would be claimed, might take many centuries.

Another related argument is concerned with specifically evaluative considerations. It runs 'We, over many centuries, have built up a cultural tradition which we value and which distinguishes us from all other people, who have their cultures which they no doubt evaluate in a similar way. We believe, however, that the mixture of cultures is not possible without corrupting both of them. On these grounds we cannot accept these outsiders as equals in our society.'

Or the argument might be put in religious and theological terms. One crude Christian doctrine asserts simply that the descendants of Noah's son Ham are visibly identifiable by their black skins and destined by divine decree to positions of inferiority in society. On a slightly more sophisticated level one hears of an English Archbishop asserting to Africans in Africa that while all men are equal in the love of God they are not necessarily equal in the sight of God, an obscure theological distinction which, in context, justifies the inequality of Africans in a mixed-race colony. Finally there is a rich range of distinctions which results from the Calvinistic notion of election. The notion of the new Israel, as consisting of individuals whom God has called, gives way very readily to the notion of ethnic groups being chosen for differing historical and political destinies.

It may be simply a matter of terminology whether or not doctrines such as these are called racist or not. Even if they were not, however, and even if the term were confined to simple, genetic theories, it might still be argued that the functional equivalence of such theories and the purely genetic ones was so great that after the sociologist had dealt with the phenomenon of racism in the narrow sense he would still have further material to analyse. The view taken here, however, is a more radical one. It is that the essence of the phenomenon of racism is to be found in all of these theories. It is important that we should see what this essence is.

In our belief the common element in all these theories is that they see the connection between membership of a particular group and of the genetically related sub-groups (i.e. families and lineages) of which that group is compounded and the possession of evaluated equalities as completely deterministic. It doesn't really matter whether this is because of men's genes, because of the history to which their ancestors have been exposed, because of the nature of their culture or because of divine decree. Whichever is the case, it might be argued that this man is an X and that, being an X, he is bound to have particular undesirable qualities. Moreover, there is nothing which he can do either for himself or for his children which can alter this situation.

This, it seems to us, is a far more important general feature of doctrines which operate in race relations situations than is the particular and historically confined doctrine of genetic difference. On the theoretical level this appeal to deterministic theory acts as a kind of equivalent to ascriptive rôle allocation on the level of policy and action. Thus we might expect that a race relations situation would always be marked by some appeal to a deterministic theory, but we should by no means expect that that theory would always be a biological or a genetic one. It might be based upon religious, cultural, historical, ideological or sociological grounds and it might be more or less adequately placed in a systematic theory of an explicit kind. Thus the mere fact that no one preaches and few accept false biological doctrines by no means implies that racism is not present.

We can now see more clearly what boundaries should be put to the field of race relations studies in sociology. They are not as clear and precise as some might wish. But the boundaries which we draw in theory can be no more and no less precise than those which exist in the world of everyday life. What we wish to say, then, is that race relations situations and problems have the following characteristics: they refer to situations in which two or more groups with distinct identities and recognisable characteristics are forced by economic or political circumstances to live together in a society. Within this they refer to situations in which there is a high degree of conflict between the groups and in which ascriptive criteria are used to mark out the members of each group in order that one group may pursue one of a number of hostile policies against the other. Finally within this group of situations true race relations situations may be said to exist when the practices of ascriptive allocation of rôles and rights referred to are justified in terms of some kind of deterministic theory, whether that theory be of a scientific, religious, cultural, historical, ideological or sociological kind and whether it is highly systematised, or exists only on the everyday level of folk wisdom or in the foreshortened factual or theoretical models presented by the media.

It is not, of course, the object of this book to make proposals as to how racism or racialism may be combatted. It may perhaps have the incidental effect of helping to combat them by showing how what appear to be new phenomena of a non-racialist non-racist kind are in fact simply the functional equivalents of phenomena which have been known before. But our main object has been a purely intellectual and theoretical one, to classify a sub-group of phenomena within the general field of sociology. Our conclusion is that there is a distinct field of race relations studies and we hope at least that our analysis of the theoretical problems involved may help to take the argument a stage further.

The nature of our definition, however, does raise some problems. Because it takes the form of stating first the necessary but not sufficient conditions of a race relations situation and only differentiates the field of race relations at the point at which racist theories are discussed, we might appear to be giving undue causal importance to theoretical and intellectual elements. This, however, is not our position. We do take the view that location within the legitimate belief and value system of a society does make racialist practice more secure and more effective, and would therefore suggest to practitioners within the race relations field that the intellectual combatting of racist theories is important to the fight against racialist policies. But we see this as part of a larger structural and political question. The problem facing those who fight on behalf of oppressed minorities is that the oppressors should not be allowed too much respectability. Just as there is a crucial breakthrough for racialism when 'respectable' and 'mainstream' politicians take up their doctrines, so also a breakthrough occurs when racialist practice appears to be put on a sounder intellectual footing. The problem is one of the legitimation of oppressive policies.

One the other hand we do not believe that the understanding of race relations, or the combatting of racialism and racism, can be wholly and satisfactorily accomplished, by looking only at theories. The theories should be thought of, as Pareto suggested, as at least in part symptoms of underlying behaviour. We must, therefore, keep at the centre of our study a concern with the structures of a pluralistic and conflictual kind which we examined in the earlier part of this book.

It may be that despite all that has been said here, there will still be those who feel that our attempt to define a separate field of race relations studies has been somewhat tenuous and that our case has not been fully sustained. We would hope that if it has not, it will at least promote other better attempts. But of one thing we are absolutely certain. For the next few centuries the problems which will preoccupy men politically more than any other will be problems which they subjectively define as problems of race and, sociology being the kind of discipline it is, any attempt to define its field without taking account of the actors' own subjective definition of the situation must be seriously inadequate. For us the study of what men take to be race relations problems is at the very centre of the study of comparative social structure.

7. A Working Paradigm for Race Relations Research*

A number of papers have appeared recently criticising an alleged paradigm for race relations research which is sometimes attributed to me personally and sometimes to the Unit which I direct. Inevitably in a field such as this the purpose of these criticisms has not been simply academic or sociological. Most usually they have been concerned with the practical political implications of certain of my articles or with their relation to one or other forms of Marxist discourse.[1] It would seem useful therefore to set out in a fairly short space the conceptual approach which I have developed over the past thirty years[2] for analysing race relations situations both in colonial and in metropolitan contexts.

For many of those approaching this field of study and of political action the very term 'race relations' gives offence, and I am often accused of being one of those within sociology

* Originally published in *Ethnic and Racial Studies*, London, January 1980.

1. I refer in particular to J. Bourne, (assisted by A. Sivanandan) 'Cheer-leaders and Ombudsmen – The Sociology of Race Relations in Britain', in *Race and Class*, Vol. xxi, No. 4, 1980; P. Gilroy, 'Managing the Underclass', *Race and Class*, Vol. xxi, No. 5, 1980; A. Green, 'Political Economy of Black Labour and the Racial Structure of the English Working Class', unpublished paper to the Centre for Contemporary Cultural Studies, Birmingham, 1980, and the review of Rex and Tomlinson, *Colonial Immigrants in a British City*, in *Sociology*, Vol. 14, No. 2, 1980, by Steve Fenton.

2. See J. Rex and R. Moore, *Race Community and Conflict*, Oxford University Press, 1967; 'The Concept of Race in Sociological Theory', in S. Zubaida (ed.), *Race and Racialism*, Tavistock, 1970; J. Rex, *Race Colonialism and the City*, Routledge and Kegan Paul, 1973; 'New Nations and Ethnic Minorities', in *Race and Class in Post-Colonial Society*, UNESCO, 1976 and 'Race Relations Theory and the Study of Migration to Advanced Industrial Societies' in J. Berting, R. Jurkovich, and F. Gever, *Problems in International Comparative Research in the Social Sciences*, Pergamon, Oxford, and J. Rex, and S. Tomlinson, *op. cit.*

who has advocated a 'race relations approach'. To this criticism my reply can be brief. I do not regard race relations as a special field of sociological study, distinguished by its concentration on the causal influence on men's behaviour of racial and genetic factors. As a member of the Experts Meeting on Racism and Race Prejudice held by UNESCO in Paris in 1967[3] I came to the conclusion that what was being discussed when we discussed race relations was a set of situations of particularly severe economic exploitation and political oppression. I suggested therefore that race relations was utterly dependent upon some form of class analysis. I did not, as Fenton[4] and others suggest, have to emancipate myself from a race relations approach. Rather, finding that there was a race relations approach largely affecting political and academic thinking, I sought to show what kinds of class situation were being discussed in these terms.[5]

It could, however, be claimed that within more general forms of class analysis, I did seek to specify more exactly both the kind of exploitation, oppression or conflict which was thought of as racial and the form which racial thinking took. Thus, I suggested that race relations situations had the following three elements:

(1) they referred to situations in which exploitation, oppression and conflict went beyond that which was normal in peaceful market situations;

(2) that the exploitation, oppression and conflict occurred between groups rather than simply between individuals;

(3) that the more powerful groups in such situations justified the ongoing system in terms of some sort of deterministic theory, of which genetic theories had, in the late nineteenth and twentieth centuries, been the principal sort.

Two points need to be made about this definition of the

3. A. Montagu, *Statement on Race*, Oxford University Press, London, 1972.
4. S. Fenton, *op. cit.*
5. This is what led to the publication of my *Race Relations in Sociological Theory* and to my contribution to the volume edited by Zubaida, *op. cit.*

field in view of subsequent criticism. The first relates to the relative causal rôle of belief systems, and the second to the meaning of exploitation beyond that occurring in peaceful market situations. On the first of these points I would insist that I am not adopting an 'idealist' position or suggesting that structures are caused by bodies of ideas. What I do claim is that, given the very severity of exploitation and oppression which exists, very strong theoretical justification is called for, and that the existence of such theoretical justification is a distinguishing mark of this particular category of social structures. I would also add that, once launched, such theoretical justifications take on a secondary life of their own, and have some causal influence. On the second point, I am aware that my distinction between exploitation in a labour market situation and exploitation which goes beyond that which is normal in the market leads to criticisms from Marxists, who would claim that this fails to understand what may be called the central point of Marxism, namely that bourgeois mystification of exploitation in the commodity form is precisely what it seeks to unmask, by showing that it is exploitation nonetheless. To this I would say that, while I fully accept that what goes on in a labour market is exploitation, nonetheless Marxists themselves have found it necessary to distinguish between capitalism at the centre, based upon concealed exploitation in the labour market, and colonial or peripheral capitalism, in which exploitation is direct and unconcealed. I do not think that in the last analysis there is justification in Marxism for opposing the distinction made by Weber between the exploitation which is normal in Occidental capitalism 'peacefully oriented to market opportunities' and the 'booty' or 'adventurer' capitalism which is normal under imperialism.[6]

If I am criticised for having adopted a 'race relations approach', because I sought to provide a sociological analysis of those situations which were called race relations situations,

6. See M. Weber, *General Economic History*, Collier-Macmillan, London, 1961.

something similar has occurred in relation to my discussion of plural society theory. When I first encountered this type of theorisation, I responded with an article which suggested that what was being discussed could be better understood in terms of political conflict theory or class analysis.[7] I saw Malinowski and Myrdal as pointing, despite their own colonialist (Malinowski) and liberal (Myrdal) approaches, in the direction of such a class analysis. Subsequently I encountered the work of M. G. Smith and suggested that his plural segments in Caribbean society could not be understood as held together only by the 'political institution'. If, however, they were united through the 'economy' they must have some of the characteristics of classes in the Marxist sense. For those who believed that sociological analysis must start from modes of production, and from there alone, however, this was not adequate.[8] Because I had sought to reanalyse pluralism, I was inevitably thought of as a pluralist.

One particular application of my critique of pluralism was in the study of South Africa.[9] There, as elsewhere, I refused to see the alleged plural segments as anything other than classes with different relations to the means of production. On this matter, however, I ran into opposition of another kind from Marxists. I had always taken and still take the view that African workers migrating between overcrowded reserves on the one hand and tightly policed municipal locations and mining compounds on the other had a different class situation from white workers enjoying considerable job security, trade union rights, welfare provisions and access to political power,

7. J. Rex, 'The Plural Society in Sociological Theory', in *British Journal of Sociology*, Vol. X, No. 2, 1959.

8. This was the theme of a review by Zubaida in the *Times Higher Education Supplement*.

9. See my *Race Colonialism and the City* and 'The Reserve, The Compound and the Location – The Three Essential Insitutions of South African Labour Exploitation' in *South African Labour Bulletin*, Vol. 1, No. 4, Durban, 1971 and 'Structural and Cultural Factors in a Liberated South Africa' in J. Rex, (ed.) *Apartheid and Social Research*, UNESCO (forthcoming).

in a racial supremacy system. This was not, however, acceptable in his earlier writings[10] to Wolpe, my South African
Marxist contemporary, who maintained that the differences
between white and black workers were stratum differences
only, since both produced and had extracted from them
surplus value. Later Wolpe was, if I understand him aright, to
change his position, drawing on the work of Poulantzas and
Carshedi to argue that, while the white workers were in part
participants in the 'collective worker', they also fulfilled some
of the 'global functions of capital'.[11] There seemed to be some
understanding in this later position, even from a narrowly
defined Marxist political economy and theory, of the point
which I had been trying to make. I was however more
interested in political sociology than political economy and
was particularly concerned with the kinds of collectivities
which might be expected to emerge as political actors in South
Africa.

When large-scale settlement by immigrant workers from
the Caribbean and South Asia became an issue in Britain, it
seemed to me that there might be similarities, even though
there were also differences, between the class relations of
white native and 'black' immigrant labour in Britain and the
relations between the two working classes in South Africa. In
order to understand this, however, it seemed to me that one
had to have a comprehensive theory of the social structure of
empire within which the basis of class formation of both
immigrant and native metropolitan worker could be located.

I had always been at pains to point out to my British
sociology students that no course which based itself purely on
the 'Social Structure of Modern Britain' could possibly be
adequate. A good example of this seemed to me to be
provided in such simple areas as the sociology of the family.
There it was commonly suggested that the normal British

10. H. Wolpe, 'Industrialisation and Race in South Africa' in S. Zubaida, *op. cit.*
11. H. Wolpe, 'The White Working Class in South Africa', *Economy and Society*,
Vol. 5, No. 2, London, 1976.

family was of the small isolated conjugal type and that this could be functionally explained as meeting the needs of British society. I argued against this that large extended families in Ireland were an essential part of British society. On even more important issues, however, it seemed clear to me that Eric Williams had shown that the British industrial revolution was crucially dependent upon wealth acquired in the triangular trade. In a very real sense the slave plantations of the Caribbean in the seventeenth and eighteenth centuries were part of the social structure of modern Britain.

I was thus led to the view that the appropriate unit of analysis for any sociologist concerned with serious macro-sociological problems was something like 'the British Empire over four hundred years'. I therefore found that I had some sympathy with the growing new trend in sociology which had developed around the work of Immanuel Wallerstein.[12] Wallerstein, it seemed to me, underplayed the importance of empires as social units in his preference for the notion of a world economic system, but I could at least agree that, with the decline of empires, there tended to be a regrouping of peripheral colonial areas around new metropolitan supra-national economic centres.

What I found agreeable in Wallerstein's book was his clear recognition of the differences between the social structures, institutions of production and forms of labour discipline at the periphery from those at the centre. The fact that he emphasised the notion of one world system did not alter this. Indeed what was most important was the recognition that one world capitalist system could generate different types of productive institutions. Wallerstein's major book, however, was historically based and dealt only with the two peripheries of the world system in the sixteenth century, namely those to be found in the plantation systems of the Americas and those

12. I. Wallerstein, *The Modern World System: Capitalist Agriculture and the Origins of the European World Economy in the Sixteenth Century*, Academic Press, New York, 1974.

represented by the so-called 'second serfdom' in Eastern Europe. What seemed to me to be needed was an extension of this sociological approach to later times and places to include, for instance, India which appears in Wallerstein's book as still beyond the periphery and, much later, to migrations from the periphery and semi-periphery to the centre.

Parallel to Wallerstein's work a debate was going on within Marxism, which was of some considerable interest. An earlier simplistic Marxism had felt it necessary to classify colonial societies in terms of what appeared to be the only categories available, namely those of feudalism and the Asiatic Mode of Production. Frank,[13] who saw himself as a Marxist, criticised such notions, pointing out that colonialism and dependency was a capitalist phenomenon. The same capitalist process which led to development at the centre was seen as producing the development of underdevelopment at the periphery.

Frank's Marxism was soon under attack from those who saw him as defining capitalism in terms of production for the market, the critics holding that a true Marxist approach must start, not from the Smithian concept of exchange, but from production. Sometimes this took the argument in a full circle leading back to the notion that colonial modes of production were feudal, but as against this there now seemed also to be another possibility, namely that a single world capitalism produced simultaneously two different sets of institutions of production. I have very little interest in the question of which of these approaches is the true Marxist one. That is a question of dogmatics and apologetics. What does seem to me to be essential at this stage is an adequate description of the variety of types of social structure to be found in the capitalism of the centre on the one hand and the capitalism of the periphery on the other. It has, after all, been in conditions of colonial capitalism, above all, that situations thought of as race relations situations have emerged and, even where they occur in

13. A. G. Frank, *The Sociology of Underdevelopment and the Underdevelopment of Sociology*, Zenith Press, Copenhagen (undated) and *Capitalism and Underdevelopment in Latin America*, Monthly Review Press, New York, 1969.

the metropolis itself, they appear to result from the interaction between the centre and periphery through migration.[14]

Before turning to my main theme which is a consideration of the variable structural elements which must be involved in an adequate sociology of colonialism there is one other point about my own work which requires clarification. This is that, however much race relations situations in the metropolis may be dependent upon the sociology of empire as a whole, this does not mean that there is no need to consider the mechanisms of assimilation and repulsion, of possible class alliance and class conflict, which actually occur in the metropolis. Thus, when I first came to write about race relations in Britain,[15] I concentrated on the study of these mechanisms. Particularly I drew attention to the way in which conflict over housing was immediately involved in the exacerbation of class conflict and empire-based conflict. There is every reason for studying such processes in detail if we are to achieve more than a purely ideological or utopian sociology, but I have made clear in many places that I by no means believe that class conflict within metropolitan capitalism, let alone housing class conflict, could possibly provide a total explanation of racial conflict.

Race relations and the social structure of empire

The starting point of a sociology of the social structure of empire and the class-like social formations to which it gives rise must lie in the distinction which has to be made between class relations of the metropolis and the class relations of the

14. See particularly R. Brenner, 'The Origins of Capitalist Development – A Critique of Neo-Smithian Marxism', in *New Left Review*, No. 104, London, 1977; J. Banarji, 'Modes of Production in a Materialist Conception of History', in *Capital and Class*, No. 3, London, 1977; and H. Alavi, 'The Colonial Mode of Production' in *Socialist Register*, 1975, and J. Rex, *Race Colonialism and the City*.

15. J. Rex and R. Moore, *Race, Community and Conflict*, Oxford University Press, London, 1967.

colonial periphery. Here I would suggest that what happens in the metropolitan centre is the exploitation within capitalism of formally free labour through a labour market. Such exploitation leads inevitably to class struggle and the attempt by the workers to defend themselves. Marx's notion of the transition from a class-in-itself to a class-for-itself helps us to formulate these problems. Nonetheless it has to be pointed out that, far from the normal process being one of revolution and a drive to a new hegemony by the exploited class, what has normally happened has been the concession to the working class, for longish periods at least, of minimum rights of collective bargaining and welfare, resulting, so long as the truce in the class war lasts, in the integration of the workers into a welfare state.[16] I certainly do not wish to claim that this is a permanent situation or that capitalism is not capable of brutal regressions at times of crisis to direct and violent exploitation and oppression of the working class. The existence of integration in the welfare state, however, does prevail for periods and distinguishes capitalism at the metropolitan centre from the forms which it takes at the colonial periphery.

Exploitation at the colonial periphery rarely involves free labour at the outset. Normally it takes one of the forms suggested by Weber in his discussion of adventurer and booty capitalism. Nonetheless there are many forms of colonial economic enterprise and we are only at the beginnings of establishing any kind of morphology of colonial social forms. What I have proposed therefore is a consideration of some of the major variable elements out of which such a morphology might be constructed.[17]

16. See T. H. Marshall, *Class, Citizenship and Social Development*, Greenwood, London, 1964. For my own views on this question see my *Key Problems of Sociological Theory*, Routledge and Kegan Paul, London, 1961.

17. See my 'New Nations and Ethnic Minorities' in the UNESCO volume cited and a more recent formulation in my contribution to a volume on Racism and Colonialism to be edited by Robert Ross for the Centre for the Study of the European Conference, Leyden (forthcoming).

It is wrong, of course, to imagine that the former colonial societies of the modern world still have their original colonial social structure. It is perhaps equally misleading, however, to think that this original colonial social structure counts for nothing, and that all social systems in the modern world can be analysed in terms of concepts appropriate for the study of modern capitalism. Our morphology of colonial societies, therefore, must be based both on the constitutive structural variables which go to the initial making of the colonial social form and upon variables of process which direct different colonies along different paths of social, economic and political development.

Naturally a morphology as such gives only a static picture. When we have elaborated it, it would still be necessary to ask what leads one social stage or social form to change or give way to another. So far as this is concerned, I believe that a Marxism less dogmatic than the kind of Marxism which we have had to deal with in the recent past would have much to contribute. On the one hand one would need a political economy of the crises and contradictions undergone by different social formations. On the other one would need a political sociology of class struggle. Not being a political economist myself I have not made any significant contribution to the former and believe that there is considerable danger in those who lack adequate knowledge of the theory of political economy rushing in to offer dogmatic explanations. So far as the political sociology of class struggle is concerned, I believe that my suggestions about a morphology, which have much to do with class formation, point the way towards the kind of social dynamics of colonial society which might be envisaged. I recognise, however, that an adequate Marxism and an adequate sociology of colonial society must bring together the analysis of economic crises and contradictions with the analysis of class conflict and change. If I emphasise class struggle at the expense of economic crisis, I do so in the hope that it may serve at least to compensate for an overemphasis in the opposite direction, which suggests that change follows directly as a matter of course from economic crisis.

Colonial and post-colonial society

Turning now to what I suppose must be the centre-piece in my own paradigm, the analysis of the basic variables involved in colonial social structure, I begin with what I call the constitutive variables. I suggest that in their formation colonial societies will vary according to the kind of pre-colonial society involved, according to the basic type of economic or labour exploitation which is established there, and according to the kind of overall stratification system which arises around the basic productive core. Having considered the kinds of variation which might be found under these headings, I shall go on to consider the variables in the processes of change which such societies undergo from economic liberalisation, from political independence, from incorporation into a wider modernising world capitalism and through internal processes of class struggle and revolution. Thus we have:

Constitutive variables:
1. Pre-colonial social forms.
2. Basic forms of colonial exploitation.
3. Systems of social stratification.

Processual variables:
1. Economic liberalisation.
2. Political independence.
3. Incorporation into world system.
4. Internal processes of class struggle and revolution.

Let us deal with each of these in turn.

Pre-colonial social forms
The social systems with which the European imperial powers made contact were by no means uniform. They ranged from

the small bands of nomadic hunters encountered by the Hudsons Bay Company in Northern Canada to the enormously complex Moghul Empire in India. Along other dimensions, one should also notice that the imperial conquerors overthrew civilisations of a more archaic if complex kind, as in Central America, and that, in the case of the West African Empires, the primary form of exploitation consisted in using existing West African institutions as a basis for building a slave trade, so that wholly new societies based on slavery could be established in the Caribbean.

European thinking about these societies was inevitably marked by the racism which grew along with the act of conquest. At first this meant that the peoples concerned were seen as essentially heathen and different, incapable without compulsion of moving into the twentieth century. Against this, a later humanitarian age insisted on the common humanity of all men, but, since the common humanity which was imputed to colonial men was the humanity of their colonial conquerors, such a view could also be infected with racism. It is worthy of note that both Marx and Weber saw economic advancement as a possibility uniquely belonging to the civilisation of the West. For Weber Hinduism was the very antithesis of the Protestant Ethic, which had made capitalism possible, while, for Marx, the British occupation of India was the only revolution which Asia ever knew.

A more balanced view would be that, while capitalism and colonialism certainly redirected the life of the societies which were conquered they were not dealing with an infinitely malleable social clay. Enslavement and transformation might, one would have thought, have involved a kind of social and cultural decimation which would make the creation of a new type of man and worker suitable for the purposes of capitalism possible, but in fact those who are descended from the original slaves have always, and increasingly in recent years, been concerned to reassert their cultural identity. The so-called Indians of the Americas proved unsuitable as workers within the plantation and factory systems and were instead marginalised on reservations. Finally, so far as the civilisations of South Asia were concerned, they continued partially to function according to their own logic, while at the same time actually participating in the colonialist and capitalist enterprise.

This relative lack of malleability is something which has to be taken into account in the systematic sociology of colonialism in three respects. It means that the variety of colonial social types is greater than would be thought if one supposed that their range was limited to the range of possible types of capitalist colonial enterprise. It means that, as they emerge from colonialism, these societies might undergo paths of development which have their own inner logic. Finally, it means that transported and migrating workers will not be simply so much dust to be blown around by capitalism either in other colonies or in the metropolis itself, but rather men, constituted by their own social and cultural systems and acting accordingly.

The basic forms of colonial exploitation
There is some disagreement amongst contemporary sociologists as to whether the different kinds of productive institution which arose in colonial situations were necessary in order that there should be an initial extraction of wealth to provide the capital for capitalist development. Marx, for example, spoke of the 'so-called period of primitive accumulation' and apparently did not think that the notion was essential to explain the emergence of capitalism. This, however, does not alter the fact that a considerable transfer of wealth actually occurred. In the periphery there were institutions of production established which involved a direct use of force and unfreedom which was not known in what came to be seen as peaceful labour markets, and there is no doubt that wealth flowed from the Americas which helped to finance English industrialisation. In Weber's terms, along with capitalism

peacefully oriented to market opportunity, there were other capitalist enterprises not limited to peaceful means, involving both high risk and violence, which he called adventurer and booty capitalism. It is this kind of capitalism which determines the range of types of productive institution in colonial society.

According to Weber the non-peaceful type of capitalist enterprise is the main type of capitalism existing in the ancient and mediaeval worlds. Existing on the margins of these societies rather than as its principle economic form, these capitalist enterprises typically seek a profit through the financing of wars and voyages, through plantation agriculture, mining and occasionally industrial production, all using unfree labour, and, finally, through tax-farming.[18]

The sociology of colonial economic production and exploitation may be seen as spelling out the detail of these various forms. The first and polar case is represented by the simple quest for booty as represented by Spanish colonial adventurers in Central America. There has to be a finite limit to such exploitation, however, and very soon it gives way to other forms based upon the direct appropriation of labour, as in the *encomienda* or in the establishment of large estates or *latifundia* with the existing occupants of the land being offered servile status.

Some such colonial forms project into colonial society the feudal ambitions of the colonialists. That is to say they seek not so much production for a monetary profit but production for immediate consumption at the lord's table with a view to enhancing his style of life and status. In a differentiated world economy, however, forms of this kind give way to production for the market and for monetary profit.[19] The central institutions of this new type of production are slave plantations and colonial mining enterprises using unfree labour. Although

18. M. Weber, *op. cit.*
19. See L. Foner and E. Genoves, *Slavery in the New World*, Prentice Hall, Engelwood Cliffs, 1969.

Weber had noted the inherent irrationalities of slavery which lay in the difficulty of finding new slaves, and in feeding existing ones in times of low demand for their products, there were long periods when such production could be not merely capitalistic, but actually enjoy a high measure of rational calculability.[20] Furthermore, as colonial experience accumulated, a variety of short-term indentures were instituted which combined the advantages of unfree labour with increasing flexibility of exploitation.[21]

Trade, of course, played its part in colonialism. The 'financing of voyages' meant, amongst other things, the possibility of buying cheap at the colonial end and making vast profits in unknown distant markets. It was also possible in negotiations with hunters and peasants to combine fraud and force as the actual price of the product was fixed in a market sustained with guns. On the other hand it would probably be a mistake to emphasise trade as such as a prime factor in colonialism. Colonial trade rested on force, and it was the institutions of production which made colonial profits possible.

The involvement of Britain with India through the East India Company exemplifies this process. The original financing of voyages produced the trade in spices and other luxuries, but such trade was not necessarily to the disadvantage of India. Exploitation came to depend much more upon the classic booty capitalist technique of tax-farming. Tax-farming, however, is a political activity which leads to government and, finally, under the new imperial peace, opportunities arise for new enterprises concerned with internal trade and industry. In the case of the later chartered companies

20. On the question of profitability see R. W. Fogel and S. Engermann, *Time on the Cross*, 2 vols, Wildwood House, New York, 1974. For an interesting example of a combination of national calculation and slavery, see R. Pares, *A West Indian Fortune*, Longmans, London, 1950.

21. On the use of indentured labour see H. Tinker, *A New System of Slavery*, Oxford University Press, London, 1974. Also my article in the *South African Labour Bulletin*, *op. cit.*

which were set up at the end of the nineteenth century for the development of Africa, most of these same elements were present, although, with a less established system of revenue collection, it was not so much the possibility of farming the revenue, but of farming and mining the land which attracted the capitalist adventurers.

It need hardly be added that the exploitation of peasants underlies nearly all colonial forms. The revenue which was farmed in India was a revenue derived from peasant rents. What is called migrant labour is the labour service of peasants, whose domestic economy does not allow them to make ends meet. Peasants living in *minifundia* on the edges of the *latifundia* are forced into labour service and sharecropping, and distinctions in status between nominally free peasants and servile squatters may well be obscure. A peasant indeed should not be thought of either as a subsistence farmer or as a farmer producing for the market only. Centrally he is a farmer who has been brought into the orbit of a larger company and is exploited by it. Capitalist enterprises which are not primarily defined as concerned with the exploitation of peasants often rest upon the farming of the peasants' surplus.

There is in any case a variety of forms of basic colonial institutions of production, each to be studied in terms of its own political economy and in terms of its own particular political sociology. Such institutions are central to the understanding of the dynamics of these societies. They do not, however, exhaustively describe them. A society is more than simply its institutions of production. What we now have to do, therefore, is to describe the social structures, which arise around the productive core and which, indeed, make its continued operation possible. That is to say we have to describe the variables involved in colonial systems of social stratification.

Systems of social stratification

In earlier attempts to formulate an adequate account of social stratification in colonial society, I have suggested that although the terms 'caste' and 'estate' are suggestive of what we observe, neither is quite adequate, particularly if the former is thought of as referring to Indian society, and the latter as referring to mediaeval Europe. More recently it has seemed to me, however, that if the term 'estate system' is taken to refer to societies in which there are not simply one class of citizens, but a number of groups with different legal rights or differing degrees of access to the law, then that term does describe what we see in all colonial societies in their constitutive period. It seems appropriate therefore to speak of colonial estate systems.

The basic owner-entrepreneurs in colonial enterprises and the categories of producers whom they exploit set the framework for the study of social stratification. Basically, the owner-entrepreneurs are free men, usually supported by the metropolitan government, while the peasants, slaves and other workers whom they exploit are unfree. No colonial society lasts for long, however, before these two basic groups are joined by others with varying degrees of freedom.

The first group to be considered are the free workers who appear on the edges of the plantations and estates and in the small colonial towns. These include freed slaves, coloureds and poor whites, in the plantation colonies, and, in countries like Mexico, Indians who have lost their own language and culture and become hispanicised. All of these groups have ambiguous status in relation to the basic polarity of freedom and unfreedom. A number of practical rules are therefore likely to be evolved in different societies, which treat these separate groups as unities or divide them up. In the United States the basic rule was that all those who were not white were grouped together as black. In South Africa an intermediate estate of coloureds was invented. Mexico at one time recognised a whole graded system of colour-castes. In some other societies this principle of grading was taken to its logical conclusion and social rights and recognition seen as depending on degree of perceived colour.

It must be noted that a system of colour estates of any of these kinds sometimes depended upon *de facto* rather than *de jure* denial or granting of rights. Nonetheless these *de facto* distinctions do represent differing degrees of right, and the term 'estate' still seems appropriate. They are the more important, moreover, because they survive as bases for distinguishing between the rights of one group and another even after emancipation brings legal equality to all.

The next group to be considered are secondary colonialists such as the Indian traders of East Africa, the Lebanese of West Africa, the Jews, Indians and Portuguese of the Caribbean. These traders did not enjoy the full backing of the metropolitan colonial power. Nor did they have access to the most lucrative economic opportunities. Nonetheless they did enjoy some protection, and, compared with the basic workers, they were free. In many colonial societies, socially and legally, they formed a third estate whose relation to the basic productive system was very like that of the merchants to the manorial economy of the middle ages. In their case, however, their racial and ethnic distinctiveness served to reinforce their legal differentiation.

The dominant metropolitan group in the colonial situation usually had some of the characteristics of what is called in American history a 'plantocracy'. It is not the case, however, that they were the only metropolitan group to be found in the colonies. The colonial situation provided opportunities for medium and large-scale capitalist farming, for a variety of forms of capitalist trading and industrial enterprise, apart from the 'pariah' opportunities taken up by aliens and, not least, for free labour, which in many industries was more rewarding than was equivalent work in the metropolis. In Marxian terms, these three groups of settlers were different classes, engaged in class struggle with one another. In fact, because of the common legal rights which they enjoyed and the associated shared style of life which went with those rights, these 'white settlers' could be thought of as a single independent estate.

White settlers, as distinct from the plantocracy, form a minor group in some colonies. There are, however, others in which the possibility exists of the colony becoming primarily a colony of settlement. Since, moreover, settler society is a free society, it has the possibility of becoming the dominating element when, for a variety of reasons, free trade becomes the norm in the economy of the empire as a whole. It is sometimes difficult, however, to make the distinction between plantocracy and settler which we are making here an absolute one, since many sections of the settler community are likely to be possessed of something very like the colonialist or booty capitalist mentality of the planters.

So far we have suggested that the metropolitan government is at one with the main owner-entrepreneurs in the colony. This cannot, however, be completely true, since long-term and short-term interests have to be reconciled, as have the interests of the plantocracy and other economic interests in the metropolis and elsewhere. In addition, the metropolitan government has to take account of the military and political implications of what its citizens do. It is necessary, therefore, that there should be installed in the colony a cadre of administrators, who remain distinct from the planters and settlers and can ensure these wider interests. Such a cadre of administrators reached its fullest development in the period of British government in India and set an ideal of behaviour to which administrators in other colonies made only a partial approximation. It need hardly be said that the administrators' own view of their rôle was a highly ideological one, and that they were never the Guardians in the Platonic sense which they claimed themselves to be. Nor were they the guardians of the indigenous colonial people. They were simply able to create this self-image because their interests and ideals were manifestly not simply those of the major exploiting classes.

Finally, one has to note one other 'estate', who share some of the characteristics of the administrators. These are the missionary clergy. Just as the administrators build up and sustain a viable political order, so the missionaries attempt to create a moral one. It is not necessary to claim either that they are the protectors of the indigenous people, or that they simply connive in their exploitation, They are the agents through whom a climate is created within which more than merely short-term selfish interests are served. Where they exist, they succeed in creating something of that common moral will whose absence in Indonesia Furnivell took to be the defining feature of the plural society.

What we have outlined so far are the variable elements out of which a number of different kinds of colonial societies come to be constructed. We now have to recognise, however, that, whatever particular forms emerge from this matrix they do not remain static. The metropolitan society undergoing capitalist development may no longer be supportive of colonial interests at later stages of its own development as it was in earlier mercantilist periods and the colonial society also has its own dynamic. Necessarily therefore all colonial societies, once constituted, undergo change. The kinds of changes which they may undergo are what we discuss under the heading of the 'processual variables'.

Economic liberalisation
It is clear that, from the beginning of the nineteenth century onwards, the theory of capitalism in Europe shifted from the theory of mercantilism to the theory of free trade. Whether this was because, to use Marxist terms, the mercantile system was no longer capable of developing production and had become a fetter on production, or whether, an initial period of exploitation and accumulation having provided the necessary capital for launching the capitalist system in Europe, further plunder of the colonies was no longer central or

essential, are questions for political economy. What certainly
is the case is that those forms of economic exploitation which
we have called 'booty capitalism', and which formed the
centre-pieces of the colonial economies during the constitutive period, no longer received the kind of backing from the
metropolis which they had received at that time, and that they
struggled to coexist with new economic forms which belonged
more naturally to the world of free trade, or simply stagnated.

The two major changes which the colonial world now
witnessed which followed from the new metropolitan economic policies were labour emancipation and land reform. The
plantation and the estate, if they were to survive, had to take
on new and modified forms and, where they did not, a new
order was born based upon free competition for jobs and for
land.

It should not be assumed that the older economic forms
were all forced to change because they were in a state of
internal crisis. In some cases this may have been so, but there
were periods in which the slave plantation system, for example, was actually a highly efficient form of production. What is
important to notice is that, even where they were internally
efficient, the overall thrust of the world system of which they
were a part had changed and that they had to struggle for
political survival.

Plantations did not, however, respond to this situation by
simply employing free wage labour. When the slave trade
became illegal, the five-year indenture system became the
norm and Indian coolies were recruited to staff what were
often highly efficient economic enterprises. To this day,
moreover, short-term contract labour of an unfree kind is the
very basis of capitalist mining and, sometimes, agriculture in
Africa. What one sees, therefore, is an adjustment of the
institutions of booty capitalism to the new economic climate
which is, at best, partial. Similarly the estate system might
make an adjustment to modern economic and political theory
and yet retain a measure of unfreedom amongst its tenants

through such institutions as sharecropping.

Outside of the plantation and estate systems a new competitive order was instituted. This new order enshrined the highest political ideals of freedom and equality of opportunity. What it could not ensure, however, was equality of outcome. It was the fate of many parts of the colonial economic system that they should simply stagnate within the new order, not necessarily being exploited within it, but simply left out of it. Nowhere is this more true than in the case of emancipated slaves who sought industrial employment in the towns. In the United States and Brazil alike, black workers saw the opportunities for employment in the new capitalist factories snapped up before their eyes by European immigrants, while they were ghettoised in Chicago, Detroit or New York or marginalised as in Sao Paulo.[22] Peasants suffered a similar fate. Lacking the capital to be able to compete as capitalist farmers they were forced into some new form of dependence, or out of farming altogether, to join the other marginalised workers in the cities.

The essential point to notice here is that the transformation of colonial society in the period of economic liberalisation is rarely complete. Colonial societies almost by definition involve internal political conflicts over the survival of old economic forms and even the new competitive forms produce types of stratification very different from those which exist in the metropolis. Even in the United States which, *prima facie*, would seem to be most like a European capitalist society (indeed, to be the capitalist society *par excellence* untrammelled by vestiges of feudalism) the forms taken in 1980 by the race relations problem are really only understandable in terms of a struggle between modern capitalist and old colonial principles. Equally, in South Africa, despite the attempt by neo-Marxist historians to argue that the racial supremacy system is necessarily and only a part of the capital-

22. See F. Fernandes, *The Negro in Brazilian Society*, Columbia University Press, New York, 1969.

ist mode of production, it is clear that what one sees involves the survival of older colonial capitalist forms.[23]

Political independence

The processes of economic liberalisation which we have just been describing may precede or may follow political independence. So far as the latter is concerned, what tends to happen with the development of the world economic system and with the internal struggle between different classes and types of economic order within the imperial and colonial system, is that either a class in colonial society becomes sufficiently politically powerful to seize control from the metropolitan power and its agents or the metropolitan power itself becomes so weakened that it can no longer sustain its political control.

In the Americas the revolution of 1776 in the United States and the nationalist revolutions led by Bolivar in Latin America were possible because a local bourgeoisie was capable of managing its own society. The revolutions cleared the way for a self-governing capitalism. Similar kinds of independence were eventually negotiated in the settler colonies, leading in the British case to the first British Commonwealth of independent settler states. After 1945, however, a new situation had arisen. The old imperial powers simply could not afford to maintain their colonies, whether there was an available heir-apparent class or segment or not. Faced with complex ethnic estate systems they simply handed over power to that class or segment most likely to be able to exercise it, though hopefully to the class or segment likely to treat neo-colonial capitalist interest most favourably.

M. G. Smith, in his analysis of plural societies, had envisaged a dismal future for the post-colonial state. In so far as the unity of such states had rested in the colonial period on

23. For a bibliography referring to this debate see H. Wright, *The Burden of the Present Liberal-Radical Controversy over South African History*, Verry, London, 1977.

the monopoly of political power by the colonialists, the withdrawal of this power would necessarily mean either anarchy and ethnic civil war or the total domination of the new society on the political level by whichever group stepped into the colonialists' shoes.

The first thing to say about this diagnosis is that it is partly true. If one looks at countries like Guyana and Malaysia, for example, it is clear that the danger of relapse into ethnic civil war is still there. Periods of stability are achieved through the 'racial' domination of one of the ethnic groups at the expense of another or through the willingness of the group which does not control power to specialise in economic and commercial activity.

In some cases, of course, the fact that the post-colonial society is a successful capitalist one, the ruling group will not simply be an economic segment at all, but a local bourgeoisie. As such it will have more subtle sanctions to deploy than Smith will allow. More generally, too, since Smith originally held to the rather indefensible view that only the political institution was shared in a plural society, one should note that economic institutions bind one segment to another and that very often the economic power order remains relatively undisturbed by the transition to independence.

More problematic are the societies where a particular ethnic group (usually the majority) has political power thrust upon it, even though, in loosely Marxist terms, it is far from being a ruling class. In these cases two things have to happen. Firstly the group itself has to organise itself through a national party which, in effect, constitutes the new nation. Secondly it has to relate itself to the economy. It does sometimes try to capture and exercise economic power itself on behalf of the people. More often than not, however, it either does not try to do this, or fails in the attempt, and then assumes the trappings of political power while actually acting on behalf of or in alliance with external neo-colonial forces.

Incorporation into the world system

I suggested above that Wallerstein was wrong in underplaying the importance of empire in the world system. Indeed what I have argued thus far is that the notions of 'empire' and 'colonies' are essential to understanding the effect within the world system of the centre on the periphery. What is important in Wallerstein, however, is his recognition that the world system continues after the collapse of the separate political empires. It seems to me that we now live in a situation in which the various former colonies no longer have a direct political, or sometimes even a direct economic, link with their old metropolises in Britain, France, Portugal, Spain, Holland or Belgium, but relate rather to various capitalist corporations, which have their headquarters in and rely for political backing on, a number of developed industrial countries. I would emphasise, however, that this system is emergent rather than complete both at the centre and at the periphery.

It should be pointed out that the structural development which I am here referring to is a new development, to be distinguished both from the first stage of the emergence of the world system, as outlined by Wallerstein, which I have referred to as the stage of imperialism and booty capitalism, and also from the phase of economic liberalisation. Those developments may all occur without the colony becoming part of a single world system. What we are now seeing, however, is the rationalisation of all the separate parts of world capitalism under the domination of a few major corporations in the commanding heights of industry and commerce scattered across the major industrial countries. Obviously this centre is a moving one, having once been located in the old imperial countries, then predominantly in the United States, with the oil-producing countries and the oil-producing corporations playing a larger and larger part.

There are, of course, still tensions and problems within the centre. While the establishing of the European Economic Community obviously benefits the multi-national corporations, as compared with a situation in which they are subject to interference by the separate member states, it is nonetheless true that there are some capitalist corporations which still rely, and prefer to rely, on the backing of national governments. Equally the EEC as such is not completely multinational and acts in conflict very often with the United States.

At the colonial end too the world system is far from complete. There are parts of the Third World which have stayed outside the development of capitalism altogether. There are parts which still function on the principles of the old booty capitalism. There are some surviving systems of production which simply stagnate and have little significance except as slack and potential for the world system. There are modernised capitalist institutions in the peripheral colonial world which have not been incorporated into the world system at all. Finally the world system itself involves a stratification of countries as well as classes which is far from stable.

It must be emphasised then that, far from the world system being an already achieved and smoothly functioning entity, what we are describing when we use the term is a tendency towards which the world might be thought to be moving. In the meanwhile the descriptive sociology of the world system involves precisely the description of structures and institutions and classes which have not yet been incorporated and the tensions to which that lack of incorporation gives rise.

Internal processes of class struggle and revolution
Nothing could be more absurd than to discuss the problems of class struggle and revolution in the post-colonial world in terms of class categories derived from the experience of European Marxism. This is true, just as much, if Marxists use the more flexible categories of the *Eighteenth Brumaire* as if they use a simpler two or three class model. Clearly there are many possible relations to the means of production in a complex social and economic and political structure which starts out as a capitalist empire and moves towards incorpora-

tion as part of a single world system. Nor can the various groups, segments and classes be easily divided between those who yield and those who extract surplus value. We need a political economy for each of a number of different ideal types of 'mode of production' and we have to realise that these are ideal types only with actual systems of production operating partly in terms of one 'mode' and partly in terms of another. (I use the term 'mode of production' here in inverted commas because I think that the actual range of structures cannot be restricted to a few well understood modes, but actually function in terms of a range of principles influenced by their historical situation as well as their present circumstances.)

The writings of Fanon,[24] Debray[25] and Segal,[26] not to mention those of Mao-Tse Tung, have all led to a questioning both of orthodox Marxist analyses of the nature of class struggle in post-colonial society, and those of Fanon at least have suggested that, prior to any internal class struggle to achieve socialism, the peoples of the colonial societies as such have to liberate themselves from the domination of the metropolis as such, including its oppressed and exploited classes. The writings of A. G. Frank and the dependency theorists also point in this direction.

Even Fanon, however, writes within a variant of a European Marxist political problematic. The classes who engage in the colonial liberation struggle are seen as middle classes, national bourgeoisie, lumpenproletariat and so on, even though they are seen as being forced to unite against the metropolitan oppressor. What the foregoing analyses suggest however is that there are groups, classes and segments of a variety of different kinds differentially related to a number of different modes of production and being united by their separate ethnicities as well as by class consciousness. If

24. F. Fanon, *The Wretched of the Earth*, Grove, London, 1965.
25. R. Debray, *Revolution in the Revolution?*, Penguin, Harmondsworth, 1964.
26. R. Segal, *The Race War*, Cape, London, 1966.

Marxist understandings of this situation also intrude on this scene they do so as important ideological distortions of the complex political sociology of colonial society. Far from Marxism being a kind of true consciousness to be contrasted with ethnic and other consciousnesses it is one ideology among others and along with ethnicity which functions to complicate the total process of group formation and conflict.

The colonial situation is also, as we have seen, one in which, from the constitutive phases onwards, there emerges a complex estate system of ethnically and functionally differentiated estates. At the outset these estates are related to one another through their differential access to the law. From an early stage, however, those who are powerfully placed explain and rationalise the system in terms of an ideology of origins of some sort. Most usually in the imperial systems this is an ideology of race. The supersession of the colonial system by one in which one of the former dominated groups takes political power by no means implies the ending of such ideologies. True, there may be an emphasis for a time on universalism in reaction to the racism of the colonial period, but so long as there are group and class conflicts to be explained and rationalised something like racist ideology is certain to survive. The post-colonial study of race relations really means the study of group and class conflict between the constituent elements of the society rationalised in terms of relatively deterministic theories of origin.

Immigrants and the metropolitan social structure

Many of the so-called race relations problems which play such a large part nowadays in the politics of the metropolitan countries are in fact problems relating to the transfer of individuals and groups, whose structural position has previously been defined in colonial terms of some kind, to positions as workers or traders into metropolitan society itself. There are in fact three major types of such population transfers. In the case with which this chapter will be most concerned, that of Great Britain, one has a society whose political system is based upon class bargaining and which has issued at least temporarily in the emergence of a welfare state. In this case immigration has occurred, both from Ireland which has had a partially colonial relationship with Britain, and from the more obviously ex-colonial societies of South Asia and the Caribbean. In the case of Northwest Europe, again, one has a number of variants of the capitalist welfare state, with the rights of workers being guaranteed by the political power of Labour, Social Democratic or Communist parties. In these cases immigration has occurred from relatively more backward or regressive social systems in the South, as well as from former colonies in North Africa, Central Africa and the Caribbean.

Finally there is the case of the United States. In this case, one has a capitalist metropolis and a formerly colonial plantation type society welded into one nation state. Instead of class politics developing in the capitalist Northern states what has happened is that political parties have emerged precisely out of the ethnic organisations through which European settler immigrants protected their interests. Although these immigrants and their organisations are in fact newer to the United States than the forced migrants of an earlier period (i.e. the plantation slaves) it is the descendants of the latter who now appear as new immigrants into the society constituted by the European settlers.

There could be many arguments over the appropriate comparabilities here between one situation and another. They focus especially on the question of Southern European immigrants to North Europe. Are they to be regarded as equivalent to the European migrants of an earlier generation to the United States? Are they to be regarded as only marginally different from their 'hosts' and capable of being absorbed in the second or third generation at least into one or other class position in the host society? Or, finally, are they to be seen as in a similar position of inferiority and ultra-exploitability as the colonial immigrants? Such questions are important because they raise the question of what kind of general theory is appropriate to the analysis of the adjustment or otherwise of all recent migrants to metropolitan society.

The analogy which is least appropriate is that between present Southern European immigrants and those who in an earlier generation migrated to the United States. Whereas the latter came to form the main labour force and to control the political system of the United States, recent migrants in Europe enter a system in which the native working class already exercises partial political control of its own welfare state system, so that the new migrants are seen as latecomers and outsiders. These recent immigrants are thus more powerless than Europeans in the United States and are, to that extent, more like colonial immigrants. They are unlike the colonial immigrant in that, coming from often neighbouring states, they do have cultural and historical links with their countries of settlement, which make their acceptance more likely. Yet, finally, it may be the case that it is in the nature of Northwest European capitalism at this stage in its development that immigrants, whether from neighbouring states or from distant colonies, are wanted simply because ultra-exploitable labour is necessary in labour-intensive industries. It may therefore be the common lot of all the recent working-class immigrants of the fifties and sixties that they will form something of an underclass[27] or sub-proletariat, whether they are from distant colonial or short-distance and culturally related points of origin. They may even share in suffering from *racist* stigmatisation and exploitation regardless of the colours of their skins.

Obviously immigrant workers relate to their society of settlement primarily through the terms of their employment

27. For a discussion of the origins and development of this concept see the footnote to Chapter One of Rex and Tomlinson, *op. cit.*

and through the industrial class struggles in which they engage on their own behalf either in conjunction with or separately from native workers. I have never wished to deny this. What I have sought to emphasise, however, is that, in the political process of class formation, there are two disjunctions possible between the situation of the immigrant worker and that of his native-born 'comrade'. The first is that the organisations of the native workers may be less than fully effective in protecting immigrants in industry. The second is that, in so far as it is through political organisations based upon trade unions that the native workers defend their interests in sectors of allocation such as housing, education, health and social insurance, this defence might not be extended to immigrant workers, even if those workers are fully protected by trade unions in industry.

It so happens that in my own empirical work I have devoted much attention to one narrow empirical problem, namely that of differential rights of differing groups within the system of housing allocation and I have found it convenient to deal with this problem when it is held in close focus in terms of a Weberian theory of class. In so far as the housing situation might be thought of as a market situation, I have, following Weber, thought it useful to speak of 'housing classes'. I have also suggested that it is possible in empirical work to consider such housing classes as operating relatively independently of 'industrial classes', 'educational classes' or 'classes' in any other sector of allocation.

Subsequently, and because I had been criticised for assuming rather than proving this disjunction, I decided, in my work with Sally Tomlinson,[28] to look at the class situation and life-chances of immigrant workers compared with those of the native-born in each of the spheres of housing, employment and education. What we found was that in each of the three spheres the situation of the immigrant partially overlapped with, partially was qualitatively separated from, that of the

28. *Ibid.*

native worker, and that the degree of overlap in one sector did not necessarily imply the same degree of overlap in another. In particular we were still inclined to the view that, however much immigrants might be integrated in the workplace (an integration which we saw in any case as only partial), this did not mean that they were accorded the same rights as their native peers in matters of residence and education.

There has been much misunderstanding about what Tomlinson and I have had to say on these matters. We did not set out to 'disprove Marxism'. Our problem in the studies mentioned was not that of the long-term political dynamics of capitalist society. Had we been discussing that, we should have needed to make an economic analysis of the long-term prospects of capitalism, in order to see whether in fact any revolutionary trend based upon the organisations of industrial workers was to be expected. One could imagine such an analysis pointing to developments in which political struggles arising from the exploitation of workers in industry came to have priority over all else. Even in such analysis, however, we should have had at some point to look at the existing structures which would be swept away by a developing revolutionary consciousness. What we have to say on those matters would therefore serve to complement rather than refute any such Marxist analysis.

Recent Marxist urban sociology, as represented by Castells and his school,[29] has of course sought to locate the allocative systems to which we have been referring with a larger institutional theory of capitalist society. Within this theory the provision of working-class housing, for example, has to be considered both as part of 'collective consumption' and as part of the 'social reproduction of labour'. Moreover this is a sophisticated theory which recognises that we are dealing not simply with simple capitalism, but with a society in which the state and the local state are all involved in the management of the economic system. I have no wish to quarrel with the idea

29. M. Castells, *The Urban Question*, MIT Press, Cambridge, Mass., 1977.

that arguments on this macro-sociological level are important. They do, however, require for their support or refutation comparative data from different places and over time and I have not myself been in a position to command such data, nor have I sought to do so. Unfortunately neither have most of my Marxist colleagues, and what they say on this level remains at the moment at the level of interesting speculation.

Again, however, the work in which I have engaged with my colleagues is not to be thought of as necessarily in conflict with these macro-theories if they prove to be true. Castells, at least, realises this, because he is concerned, not simply with problems of system contradiction in the urban system, but also with political conflict in which the actors are what he calls social movements. What my own work on metropolitan societies may be construed as doing is precisely looking at some of the immediate empirical origins of such social movements.

I have, in developing such accounts, however, always found it useful to develop my ideas within a framework which can loosely be related to the Marxian notions of 'class-in-itself' and 'class-for-itself'. Consideration of relative life-chances in the different sectors of allocation may be thought of as falling under the heading of 'class-in-itself'. The actual forms of organisation which come into being, the kinds of consciousness and identity which prevail amongst the groups with these various life-chances, constitutes the world of 'class-for-itself'. Of course, according to the strict letter of Marxist theory, this term should be reserved for those situations, and those situations only, in which an oppressed class sees itself as in conflict with an oppressor class and also seeks to establish its own hegemony. If this is the case, however, at least there is a need to study the actual forms of consciousness and group organisation which do exist, prior to the full development of the 'class-in-itself'.

That identification with other industrial workers who are similarly placed is likely to constitute one of the primary forms of identity and group consciousness goes without saying. This is undoubtedly true of immigrant as of other workers, and all the evidence from Europe shows a high degree of identification of immigrant workers with the trade union movement as well as with workers' parties. What I have sought to emphasise, however, is that, whereas class identification and class organisation arising from this source provides the basis for group action in all fields for most native workers, it is characteristic of immigrant workers that their ethnic organisations, often based upon the residential community, form an alternative focus of loyalty and a basis for collective action. Class and ethnic community organisation thus become alternative bases for immigrant organisation. Since community organisation is often related to differential housing rights it cannot be dismissed as a form of false consciousness.

When one looks at the political consciousness of immigrants, however, there is another even more important factor to be noted. This is the reference to the affairs of their homelands in much of their organised activity. In England, if one looks at the Indian community one finds that one of its main organisations, namely the Indian Workers' Association, is not purely and simply a trade union for Indian workers, though it is that, but also an organisation which is concerned with the revolutionary transformation of *colonial* society. Still more significantly a great deal of West Indian political activity is not concerned simply with worker rights or even conflicts with the local police. It is very much concerned with finding ways of undoing the wrongs done by 'four hundred years of slavery'. In short, such organisations are not to be explained in terms of a class theory related only to the internal dynamics of metropolitan capitalism. They have to be understood as reflecting (a) the *special* interests of immigrant workers in metropolitan society, and (b) the role of immigrant workers, their ethnic groups and their nations, within the changing and conflictual class system, which is the social structure of empire

222

and of the world economic system.

One thing which is now becoming increasingly evident is that, after a period in which they took in substantial numbers of immigrant workers to do unwanted work, the advanced capitalist societies have begun to restrict such immigration. Industry has tended to become more capital-intensive with the development of automation and micro-processing, so far as the metropolis was concerned, but more labour-intensive industries have moved to the periphery and the former colonies. Under a new neo-colonial dispensation more and more areas of the world have been brought under the control of metropolitan industrial capitalism and into a single world system.

Class analysis and other approaches to the study of race relations

It should be clear from all that has been said above that my approach to the study of 'race relations' both in the metropolis and in the colonies is by way of an emprical class analysis. At the metropolitan end I have tried to emphasise both those tendencies which bring immigrants into the developing class struggle of the metropolis and those which involve the maintenance of ties with the homeland and the pursuit of special interests within metropolitan capitalism. To some extent any such analysis must deal in ideal types. These types serve to indicate tendencies and to provide the necessary indices in terms of which the actual empirical location of a class or ethnic group can be established.

One important criticism of my work has been that of Van den Berghe,[30] who claims that the West Indian and Asian groups which I have described are not in fact classes but what he calls 'ethnies'. I think there is something in this. I would not want to claim that all that can be said about, say, Indian

30. Review in *Contemporary Sociology*, 1981, *op. cit.*, p. xvii

immigrant behaviour, has been said when we describe the Indians as a class or underclass. There are such things as cultural peculiarities. I am not sure, however, that what is presented by the Indians to British society is simply a distinctive ethnicity. Rather it is a sub-national ethnicity which has come to play a class-like rôle in colonial society. If Van den Berghe is right to remind me of an element which depends on sheer ethnicity underlying the class behaviour of Indian workers, I think I might equally remind him of the class element underlying apparent ethnicity both in the metropolis and in colonial situations.

Perhaps more to the point is the criticism that it is an oversimplification which represents all immigrant workers as simply an 'underclass'. Probably most immigrants do enter metropolitan societies from the former colonies in such positions. That is certainly the case with the descendants of slaves from the plantation colonies and the poorest of peasants. It is also true of a great many colonial immigrants who are forced to accept employment which is beneath their level of qualification. But it is wrong to see colonial society as consisting only of teeming or huddled masses of the poor. Such societies often have complex structures and those in positions of relative privilege may use immigration as a means of enhancing their position in the homeland or as a way of finding new fields in which to exercise their skills, find profit and even of exercising power. Thus, while the mass of South Asian workers in Britain are in low-grade industrial occupations, there is a considerable development of shop-keeping, of penetration of the professions and of fairly large-scale trading activity.[31] A more refined model of colonial immigration, therefore, would necessarily have to deal with those interactions between colonial immigrants and metropolitan society which did not occur at the very bottom in underclass situations.

31. See S. Nowikowski, 'Surburban Asians', unpublished PhD thesis for the University of Manchester.

While the sorts of class analysis which I have proposed does exclude naive attempts to explain the situation of immigrant workers in terms simply of 'strangeness', it by no means excludes some other themes which have traditionally played their part in race relations theory. There is, for example, a great deal to be said for the approach of Richard Schermerhorn,[32] who has done much to categorise the formal aspects of majority-minority situations, as there is for those, like Gordon[33] and Yinger,[34] who have made useful distinctions between the various aspects of social and cultural assimilation, accommodation and so on. I would even be prepared to agree that a typology of the processes which they describe without reference to class might well draw attention to a further range of interethnic problems. With that said, however, I would suggest that in actual empirical and historical contexts, such processes operate in conjunction with class rather than separately from it.

Finally, while disagreeing with that approach which suggested that racism is a factor totally independent of class, causing men to act in contradiction of their class interests, I would certainly agree that, once racist ideology emerges as a means of justifying opposition, conflict or exploitation, it can take on a life of its own and begin to operate as an additional factor, determining the nature of group boundaries, and promoting group conflict both within, and independently of, classes. Because it has this degree of independence, an important sub-area within the sociology of race relations is that which deals with the production and dissemination of racist ideas.[35] The only position to which I would take exception is that which seeks to explain race relations situations

32. R. Schermerhorn, *Comparative Ethnic Relations*, Random House, New York, 1970.

33. M. Gordon, *Assimilation in American Life: The Role of Race Religion and National Origins*, Oxford University Press, London, 1964.

34. M. Yinger, 'Toward a Theory of Assimilation', paper presented to the International Sociological Association, Uppsala, 1978.

35. See Chapter Six of the present volume.

solely as the consequence of racist ideas and prejudice. This is a common illusion of liberal sociology and it was this essentially ideological belief which lay at the heart of a series of interventions on this question by UNESCO. It is interesting, however, that the 1967 Experts Committee at UNESCO, of which I was a member, went out of its way to emphasise the close relationship between racism and structural factors.[36]

Conclusion

I would hope that this somewhat comprehensive discussion of the ground to be covered in the sociology of race relations will serve to clarify my own position to those whose knowledge of it has depended on one or other of my empirical or theoretical essays or upon reports of what I have said by my critics. I do not wish to claim that what I have outlined is a theory of race relations. Such a theory is still a long way away. What I do believe, however, is that no theory will ever be arrived at until we have an adequate typology of structures, which is what I have sought to provide.

Finally, I should like to emphasise that my thinking on race relations is aimed neither at control of minorities, nor at developing sociological theories and definitions for their own sake.[37] The issues which I have sought to explicate are those which inevitably occur to those who seek to promote racial structural change. Rather surprisingly there are those who believe that any such writing can only have reactionary intent. For my part, while I do not see sociology as of itself a kind of political action, I would urge in this day and age a reversal of Marx's Eleventh Thesis. Recently many radicals have sought to change the world without understanding it. Sociology, it seems to me, may help to guide those with the necessary courage and resolution to more effective political action.

36. See A. Montagu, *op. cit.*
37. See J. Bourne, *op. cit.*

Index

acculturation in colonial societies, *see* missionaries, colonialism

Africa, 13, 23, 34, 40, 45, 50, 56, 72, 76, 78, 80, 101, 104; *see also* Union of South Africa, colonialism

Alavi, H., 'The Colonial Mode of Production', 169n

aldeiamentos, in Brazil, 78

Algeria, 74–5, 110

America, *see* Latin America, United States

Annan, N., 81–2; *Kipling's Place in the History of Ideas*, 82n

anti-semitism, 6, 119, 128, 131, 136

apartheid, 53

Aquinas, Thomas, 154

ascriptive rôle allocation, 114, 117–21, 126, 131, 134; particularistic, 141–2; classificatory, 142; and determinism, 159

Ashley, M., *Statement on Race*, viiin

Asia, 13, 20, 34, 72, 101

Banarji, J., 'Modes of Production in a Materialist Conception of History', x, 169n

Banton, M., *Race Relations*, xiiin; in *New Society*, 6n

barbarians, the, 34, 35, 52

beliefs, rôle of in race relations, 7–8, 133–4, 143, 150–51; and mass media, 158

belief systems, and social structures, 8, 9–10; of slavery, 46; deterministic, 86, 115; and religion, 152; and culture, 152; and social

science, 153; *see also* value systems

Bell, Daniel, 90; *End of Ideology*, 90 and n

Bendix, R., 33; *Max Weber, An Intellectual Portrait*, 33n

Bendix, R., and S.M. Lipset, *Class, Status and Power*, 60n, 61n, 62n

Berger, B. L. and T. Luckman, *The Social Construction of Reality*, 138 and n

Berting, J., F. Geyer and R. Jurkovich, *Problems of International Comparative Research in the Social Sciences*, xiii, 162n

Black Power, 111–13, 114

Bolivar, S., 184

Bott, Elizabeth, 65; *Family and Social Network*, 65n

Bourne, J., 'The Sociology of Race Relations in Britain', 162n, 199n

Boxer, C. R., 80; *Race Relations in the Portuguese Colonial Empire, 1415–1825*, 80n

Braudel, F., ix

Brazil, 49, 77, 78, 79–80, 183; and 'Big House' system, 49–50

Brenner, R., 'The Origins of Capitalist Development', x, 169n

British Guiana, 25, 55

Burma, 19

Canada, 101

Cape Coloureds, *see* Union of South Africa

capitalist system, 15, 91, 92, 93, 94, 95; Western European, 33, 34, 81, 181–2; and colonialism, 37,